D0184753

# GIDEON HAIGH

# Stroke of Genius

Victor Trumper and the shot
that changed cricket

**SIMON &
SCHUSTER**

London · New York · Sydney · Toronto · New Delhi

A CBS COMPANY

First published in Great Britain by Simon & Schuster UK Ltd, 2016
A CBS COMPANY

1 3 5 7 9 10 8 6 4 2

Simon & Schuster UK Ltd
1st Floor
222 Gray's Inn Road
London WC1X 8HB

www.simonandschuster.co.uk
www.simonandschuster.com.au
www.simonandschuster.co.in

Simon & Schuster Australia, Sydney
Simon & Schuster India, New Delhi

The author and publishers have made all reasonable efforts to contact copyright-holders
for permission, and apologise for any omissions or errors in the form of credits given.
Corrections may be made to future printings.

A CIP catalogue record for this book is available from the British Library

Hardback ISBN: 978-1-4711-4680-0
eBook ISBN: 978-1-4711-4681-7

Text design by Samantha Jayaweera © Penguin Random House Australia Pty Ltd

Printed and bound by CPI Group (UK) Ltd, Croydon, CR0 4YY

Simon & Schuster UK Ltd are committed to sourcing paper that is made from wood
grown in sustainable forests and support the Forest Stewardship Council, the leading
international forest certification organisation. Our books displaying the FSC logo are
printed on FSC certified paper.

# CONTENTS

# INTRODUCTION

The batsman appears almost airborne. Only the instep of his back foot remains grounded; the front foot hovers in space, destined never to land. Yet there is no sense of strain – only energy and expectation.

His figure is spread, as if involved in a Vitruvian exploration of batting's physical limits. His bat, slim, loosely gripped, is at the commencement of its downswing. The muscles of his left forearm are taut with pent-up power. His cap is tugged low, accentuating the precision of the gaze.

His clothing is generous, yet contoured to the hips and shoulders, expressing their purposeful geometry. His sleeves are folded just so, distinctively below the elbow, a personal signature. His legs are lightly sheathed in slatted pads, but they're purely for form's sake. All that matters is the imminent interaction of the bat with a ball we're left to imagine. Nor are there fielders, stumps, crowd. Rather is he fringed by a full-grown wattle, in the corner of a vineyard.

For I am regarding not a photograph but a statue. A hundred years after the death of Victor Trumper, I've inched my way along Victoria's Mornington Peninsula to Red Hill in search of a 2.5-metre-tall bronze cast of him – to be precise of an image of him, perhaps the most famous image in all of cricket, and certainly the image famous longest.

Crafted in 1999 by the sculptor Louis Laumen at one and a quarter times lifesize, it was acquired through the auction house

Bronzed Aussie: Trumper by Louis Laumen.

Christie's by a successful bookmaker, David McLachlan. For almost as long as he has been the owner, McLachlan has been wondering what to do with it. He has no interest in cricket; he acquired it as an investment, during a dabble in collecting. Having twice failed to sell it, he lent the statue to a developer friend, Neil Bryson, who owned a vineyard with its own little cricket ground. For a few years it provided a talking point for guests at an annual match for Bryson's friends. The statue moved to its present whereabouts, by truck and crane, when that property was sold.

Other plans have come to McLachlan's quicksilver mind from time to time. Some have been grand, such as placing it in the forecourt of a residential development to be called Trumper Towers. Some have been more rococo, like drilling a hole in the sculpture's head and turning it into a swimming-pool water feature. More recently, he's thought differently. 'For a while, I was a bit embarrassed about it,' McLachlan says. 'I'd bought it to make a few grand and it was kind of a failure.' Then a note of surprise enters his voice. 'But I've got to admit, I've fallen in love with it.'

•

For more than a century, cricket's votaries have been doing the same, at first because of who the image depicted in its original two dimensions, increasingly because of what it has become – according to sources as diverse as *Wisden Cricketers' Almanack* and Wikipedia, an 'icon'.

Victor Trumper would have been an iconic figure anyway. He was the first truly Australian sporting hero, in the sense of having an actual nation to represent, and being the best at the sport that to his countrymen mattered above all. He also formed part of a profound moral and aesthetic revaluation of cricket, an awakening to its potential beauties, an invitation to appreciations deeper than runs and wickets, victory and defeat. And after his death, he became the first Australian athlete around whom a truly lasting legend was built, remaining lodged in public affection even through decades of Bradmania, despite there being no significant book about him, no public monument to him of any description, no all-encompassing mass media to inundate the senses with messages of his greatness.

What existed, however, was this photograph – the most durable, and still among the most popular, of a great sportsman in action. Trumper remains accessible through certain canonical writings –

moving elegies in the autobiographies of teammates Monty Noble and Frank Iredale, lavish panegyrics among the works of Sir Neville Cardus and Jack Fingleton. Yet Trumper is the earliest sporting luminary to have been, in the main, visually bequeathed: he is as much his picture as Sir Donald Bradman his statistics, and perhaps even more so, as what first illuminated then complemented Trumper has almost replaced him altogether, culminating in its final transfiguration into an art object, inspiring paintings, prints, plates and figurines, helping to sell beverages and bands alike.

Despite this, the achievement of the image's creator, George Beldam, an accomplished amateur batsman and self-taught photographer, has languished in near-total neglect. He was the first skilled practitioner to devote concerted attention to sport, speaking of 'Action Photography' decades before the expression enjoyed widespread usage, and his picture of Trumper predates by generations those Australian sporting images that vie with it for fame, such as the climax of the Tied Test (Ron Lovitt), Norm Provan and Arthur Summons at the SCG in 1963 (John O'Grady) and Nicky Winmar at Victoria Park thirty years later (Wayne Ludbey).

By subordinating text to illustration, Beldam's books *Great Batsmen* and *Great Bowlers and Fielders*, in which Trumper and scores of his contemporaries go through their paces, completely reversed sport's traditional descriptive economy. Then, almost as quickly, Beldam diverted his autodidact's gaze to competing enthusiasms. A photogravure of what was originally 'Plate XXVII: Jumping out for a straight drive' on page 124 of *Great Batsmen* hangs in Australia's National Portrait Gallery; artworks derived from other of his photographs hang in Britain's. Yet Beldam's oeuvre remains uncurated and uncatalogued; a sizeable proportion of his plates have never even been printed.

Partly in consequence, it remains a mystery how the paths of Trumper and Beldam originally interleaved. None of the photographs Beldam took of Trumper are dated; neither man recorded impressions of the experience; the original of 'Jumping Out' appears to have been destroyed, accidentally, by Beldam's youngest son. Mind you, when versions have reached the scale of a quarter of a tonne of silicon bronze reinforced by steel rods, that loss hardly seems so injurious. And that the image marks no special innings and relates to no particular match may account for some of its durability: it conjures an era, an attitude; it both harks back to cricket's first visual imaginings of itself and anticipates a present day where action can be arrested by a keystroke. That front foot is still to land, just as there is always, in cricket, something about to happen.

•

Although this book has biographical elements, it is not a biography of Trumper. Three biographies give chronologies of his life, collate reportage of his innings and sentiment about his personality. *Stroke of Genius* is instead, for want of a better word, an iconography, a study of Trumper's valence in cricket's mythology and imagery. E. B. White famously likened humour to a frog: 'Humor can be dissected, as a frog can, but the thing dies in the process.' The same risk may be thought to apply to sporting legend. That's far from my purpose: on the contrary, Trumper's is a legend to which I have been attached as long as I can remember.

Like many people, I encountered Trumper and 'Jumping Out' simultaneously – in my case on page 89 of one of my earliest cricket books, a slim paperback called *Great Australian Cricket Pictures* (1975). The reproduction was poor, the caption terse and uninformative. But to it I went back and back, as can be judged from the fact that my copy today falls open at exactly that page. Such a dashing stroke. Such a vivid image. Such a musical name, too. Neville Cardus wondered aloud about the rightness or otherwise of cricketers' names after reading an evening stop press of a good score by a Worcestershire wicketkeeper called Gaukrodger: 'With such a name he ought never in this world to have been permitted to score 19, let alone 91.' It gave him a renewed appreciation of his schoolboy hero: 'Had Trumper been named Obadiah he could scarcely have scored a century for Australia against England before lunch.'*

Fittingly, it was Cardus whom I first read at length on the subject of Trumper, which again I can date exactly: a chapter from *Cricket: The Great Ones* (1967) republished in the souvenir program for 1977's Centenary Test. 'I have never met a cricketer,' began Cardus, 'who, having seen and played with Victor Trumper, did not describe him without doubt or hesitation as the most accomplished of all batsmen of his acquaintance.' No doubt or hesitation in Cardus's assertion either, nor in this later personal cameo:

As a schoolboy I at once worshipped him. He looked so like every schoolboy's idea of the perfect batsman, not too muscular; he was

---

* Others have liked the name too. Characters called 'Trumper' appear in works by cricket-loving novelists George Lamming and Jeffrey Archer. More recently, 'Victor Trumper' was a villain in the BBC's Victorian melodrama *Ripper Street* (2012), a wink from cricket-loving creator Richard Warlow.

Cricket-loving composer Tim Rice has made two uses. 'Victor Trumper' was his pseudonym for an American novelty single with MCA, 'The President Song' (1974), in which Rice recited the name of each president to a backing track, leaving a brief echo-laden silence after each one who had died violently. MCA's enthusiasm waned when a Boston radio station interpreted the silence after the name of Richard Nixon as inciting an assassination attempt. Rice's American champion in the musical *Chess* (1986) was then 'Freddie Trumper', while his right-hand man, 'Walter de Courcey', was named for Jimmy de Courcy, Australian batsman of the 1950s.

actually slender of build, but good looking of face, and of graceful movement. The problem which worried me as a schoolboy arose from the fact he was an Australian.

Every schoolboy is fanatically eager to see and to know England has beaten Australia. I would pray at my bedside at night for an England victory. Yet I always hoped Victor would play a great innings every time. A predicament! Inspiration descended on me, solving my problem. I prayed thus: 'Please God, let Victor Trumper score a century against England tomorrow . . . out of an Australian all-out score of 124.'

To an impressionable eleven-year-old, this passage opened worlds. I was a schoolboy eavesdropping on the thoughts of another schoolboy three-quarters of a century earlier. I was also encountering, for the first time, the notion of the cricketer who defies the obvious bounds of affiliation, whose success is transcendently enjoyable. In hindsight, despite being a diffident mediocrity of a cricketer, as unlike Trumper as it is possible to be, I was well on the way to naming my cat after him twenty years later.

Revisiting those foundational documents of my interest in Trumper, I am struck by different things. In *Great Australian Cricket Pictures*, 'Jumping Out' is the only photograph of a cricketer in motion before Bodyline: a comment on the abiding challenge of reviving athletes long dead and spottily recorded for a modern visual audience. In that well-thumbed *Centenary Test Souvenir*, I can see that four cricketers were deemed worthy of profile articles: Sir Donald Bradman, W. G. Grace and Sir Jack Hobbs as well as Trumper, all batsmen, all at least thirty years or so out of the game. The programme depicted their modern heirs more strikingly in advertisements: breaking up Cardus's black-and-white

Trumper was a full-colour page of Tony Greig eating Nutri-Grain. This tension 'twixt old and new was uneasier than the game's governors understood. A few months later it would be revealed that Greig among many others had been recruited during the Centenary Test by the agents of Kerry Packer for a brash new private venture, World Series Cricket. The first public act of the captain of Australia's 'establishment team', Bob Simpson, was to place a New South Wales Cricket Association (NSWCA) wreath on the grave of Victor Trumper, on the occasion of the centenary of his birth, 2 November 1977.

It went unnoted that this gesture, apparently affirming of cricket's loftiest traditions, contained an acute historical irony. For the second half of Trumper's career, he and his leading contemporaries had been at more or less permanent loggerheads with the NSWCA, which dominated Australia's inchoate Board of Control. The association at one stage banned recalcitrant players, including Trumper, in much the same way as the authorities in 1977 banned those players aligned with the Packer organisation. Far from being a period innocent in the ways of commerce, cricket in the time of Trumper could be as rapacious and fractious as our own.

Yet historical ironies are eluding us all the time, for it is not facts we find compelling so much as ideas, not the matter of achievement so much as the manner. Australians are expert at creating continuities, sidestepping complications, refurbishing traditions that suit us, neglecting those that do not. And what lingers vestigially in 'Jumping Out' is Australia's oldest cricket myth – Trumper was an idol figuratively long before he became one literally, and was acquired by a man who had never heard of him.

•

Trumper, as we shall see, is an elusive historical figure. He left no memoirs. He left no papers. He gave next to no interviews, made few public statements. Basic biographical information about him is missing. He was lauded as the most exhilarating batsman of his time, and loved as the foremost sportsman, described by contemporaries in almost Christlike terms for his modesty and selflessness. This subtly deepened his enigma. 'He was a hard man to know, because he made you so indebted to him for many kindnesses extended,' thought his teammate Frank Iredale. It also left nothing to adulterate or distract from his sporting reputation. Part of Beldam's success lay in capturing an image of comparable purity, full of what his *Great Batsmen* collaborator C. B. Fry referred to as Trumper's 'generous abandon'. The expressive photograph, argues the philosopher John Berger, works dialectically: it both 'preserves the particularity of the event recorded' and 'chooses an instant when the correspondences of those particular appearances articulate a general idea'. Beldam captured the idea of Trumper for generations to hand on, and it has endured into the era of Instagram.

It has had, as we shall see, numerous admirers, from Dennis Lillee to Steve Waugh, Sir Donald Bradman to Sir Michael Parkinson, all of whom hung it on their walls – Bradman's contemporary Jack Fingleton, his era's leading Australian cricket writer, would argue that 'Jumping Out' should hang in every cricket pavilion in all the world, an essay in elegance, an injunction to action. Its ubiquity persists. During the writing of this book, perhaps for having half an eye out for it all the while, I have seemed to encounter it everywhere – in the headquarters of the cricket equipment maker Gray-Nicolls in Melbourne's Cheltenham, on a museum wall at The Oval in London, in the pavilion at the Cricket Club of India's Brabourne Stadium in Mumbai, in a meeting room at the investment company

Insta-Vic: Trumper via the National Portrait Gallery.

Wellington Management in Boston. In October 2015, *Cricinfo* published a lengthy profile of A. B. de Villiers, probably the world's most admired cricketer, illustrated with a photograph of de Villiers from side-on, taking a huge stride, bat upraised. 'Victor Trumper would have been proud,' read the caption: few readers would have needed further elaboration. Now I recall a reproduction hung in the chambers of my late friend Michael Shatin QC, who recruited me for the cricket club where I'm now a life member. *Now I recall* ... who knows on what we might stumble in rummaging the locker of memory?

If David McLachlan knows precious little of cricket, John Goff, now a retired farmer in Tamworth, knows a good deal. He can remember when it started, too. In June 1948, he was a boy at Chatswood West Public School whose class had just graduated to ink pens. His teacher Miss Pennington, a small but severe spinster, was encouraging their efforts by caning everyone who made a blot. John was in line for encouragement again one day when he raised his hand so she could not reach, and for this was sent for additional chastisement to the headmaster's office. A kindly man, the headmaster limited the penalty to John's having to sit outside said office at lunchtime for a week.

On the opposite wall was a photograph, old and faded but thrilling, of a batsman jumping out to drive. There was nothing for seven-year-old John to do but stare at that photograph, the storming front foot and the brandished bat against the murky skyline, and the faded name underneath it: 'Victor Trumper'. It sounded vaguely familiar: a pavilion bore the same name at nearby Chatswood Oval; in fact, Trumper had been a local resident and player. Well, whomever he was, John decided, *that* was the way to bat, with a hawk eye and a headlong launch. At Chatswood West Public School, cricket was played with a crude bat and a tennis ball, and special fame awaited anyone who could hit over a two-storey building that segregated the boys' play area from the girls'. When next he was free to do so, John succeeded. It earned him another week outside the headmaster's office. More time to study the photograph – till he knew every lineament and shade.

Chatswood West shaped John Goff's life. He became a teacher, headmaster and administrator, dedicating forty-two years to the

New South Wales Education Department. He also never forgot Trumper's pictorial example. Whether in the bush on his early teaching rounds, or during the more than 300 games he played for Lane Cove CC in Sydney's Shires competition, he hit hard, straight and often. His son Jeremy, who introduced us, has childhood memories of watching his father hit six after soaring six at suburban parks on the North Shore through the 1970s. 'I always thought that was the way to play cricket,' said John when we talked. And despite never having done it that way, I had to agree.

# I

# 'THE MEMORABLY PERCEIVED PHASE'

'My great aim is to discover whether this splendid game is or is not connected with some of the beautiful laws of motion as to deserve the appellation of a science; and if so to institute a few inquiries to ascertain what are the laws that regulate such honourable appellation.'
– NICHOLAS FELIX, *Felix on the Bat* (1845)

Cricket was devised to be played, not watched. Much of the action occurs very fast, almost all of it very far from the spectator. In the twenty-first century we take for granted television's enrichment of our visual experience, how it effectively imbues us with super-human powers of perception: the profusion of powerful cameras that draw us into the centre of the action from every angle, includ-ing from through the middle stump and the umpire's hat; the pitch microphones that permit our eavesdropping on every grunt and oath; the multiplicity of replays that turn back and slow down time for our delectation; the super slo-mos that decrypt the most complex skills, and are now used so indiscriminately that fielders simply bending down to pick up a ball can appear to have been choreographed by Sam Peckinpah; above all, perhaps, the Decision Review System, augmented by Hawk Eye, Hot Spot and Snickometer, now forming cricket's ultimate appeals court. But the chief purpose of the foregoing is to counteract the obstacles that speed and distance place in the way of watching, interpreting and adjudicating cricket.

Now consider cricket without all this. To obtain a sense of it, a good place to begin is at Lord's. In the collections of the Marylebone Cricket Club is a single 28 cm × 33 cm page from the notebook of a Surrey cricketer, George Shepheard Snr, featuring watercolour sketches of a dozen prominent players of about two and a quarter centuries ago. They are the oldest surviving images of cricketers involved in an actual match, striking what the artist has called 'characteristic attitudes', such as taking block, crouching in the field, leaning on their bats. The only hint of technique is in the cameo of the eminent Hambledonian David Harris, who appears to be taking aim preparatory to an underarm delivery. The images are precious precisely because of their rarity; they also attest the elusiveness of cricket 'action'. The colours are soft, the brush-strokes quick and delicate. But hits, deliveries, catches? For even the raciest recording media, these were too fleeting and far off. In his enchanting chronicle of Hambledon, *Cricketers of My Time* (1832), Richard Nyren paused over Silver Billy Beldham to elucidate the visual treat of his batting: 'It was a study for Phidias to see Beldham rise to strike. The grandeur of the attitude, the settled composure of the look, the piercing lightning of the eye, the rapid glance of the bat, were electrical. Men's hearts throbbed within them, their cheeks turned pale and red. Michael Angelo should have painted him.' But he didn't. Nobody did.

Because it was difficult to capture moments, artists preferred to gather up games in topographic views, positioning cricketers in meadows, on greens, by churches and cathedrals; then, as cricket began drawing crowds, amid onlookers too. By the 1830s and 1840s, as illustration was democratised by new printmaking technologies and 'art' ceased to be the prerogative of the wealthy, these conventions in cricket were well established. In probably the finest and certainly the most popular example, 'A Cricket Match between the Counties of Sussex and Kent, at Brighton' (1849), the game is a backdrop to the crowd – although what a crowd. Brainchild of W. H. Mason, an occasional cricketer who expanded his Brighton stationery prem- ises into a 'Repository of Art', it features portraits of no fewer than seventy-one individuals – selected, interviewed, sketched, painted separately then grouped together by artists William Drummond and Charles Basebe, and finally engraved on copper by George Henry

Madding crowd: Mason's 'A Cricket Match'.

3

Phillips. Six years in the making, some of the subjects were dead by the time it appeared.

It is as much a social as a sporting study. While the XIs represent the finest flower of their era, we are left in no doubt that the likes of bowler William Lillywhite, a bricklayer, and batsman Fuller Pilch, a tailor, appear by the grace of the Earls, Sirs, Hons and Esqs posed languidly in the foreground. The detailed skyline, meantime, attests Brighton's burgeoning as a seaside resort thanks to royal patronage and rail service. Yet the most fascinating feature of 'A Cricket Match' became its sheer ubiquity, in original and pirated versions. The anti-quarian Alfred Taylor, who spent a lifetime researching the print and its variations, noted its hanging in 'every clubhouse in the king-dom' and beyond, from 'the wilds of northern Canada' to 'the wastes of Western Australia'. His classic monograph, *The Story of a Cricket Picture* (1923), rejoiced in tales of its fame:

> A Brighton youth wishing to experiment in a newer and brighter land was financed by his parents and packed off to Australia when immigration was at fever heat. Sad to relate, misfortune dogged his footsteps; but one eventful day he entered a saloon in Ballaret [sic], with scarcely a sou in his possession, and noted the familiar engraving in a prominent position. Only natural that he should be lost in contemplation. 'Good old Brighton,' he muttered. 'Know it?' queried the proprietor. 'Know it! My people live within the shadow of that church,' he said, pointing to the edifice of St Peter.
>
> The rest can be gathered. A freemasonry was established, and the traveller helped on his way. This time he made good, and in after years returned to Brighton a wealthy man, where he spent the remainder of his life, and where he never tired of telling the story related.

What enchanted Taylor most was his tale's testament to public suggestibility. For the match depicted never took place: that is, while the players all represented their respective counties, they never took the field against one another in these specific formations. Yet due to its sheer familiarity, Taylor encountered an 'astonishing number of old gentlemen' who claimed to have been eyewitnesses to the occasion – adamantly so, and in spite of all evidence to the contrary. One man wrote claiming to have inherited the ball; another claimed that his father had been at all three days of the match, and enclosed 'a cutting from an old newspaper' to prove it. Taylor recalled: 'Modesty forbade me to mention that same was from the defunct *Sussex Evening Times* of thirty years ago, had nothing to do with the imaginary match, and was penned by yours truly.' Even when the image was relatively scarce, perhaps even *because* it was relatively scarce, visual 'evidence' already had a cut-through to which print could only aspire. In its way, then, 'A Cricket Match' also anticipated 'Jumping Out', which likewise would decorate pavilions round the world, and likewise convince observers of its absolute verisimilitude.

•

While action lurked beyond the reach of illustrators, some groped for it, introducing a semblance of animation to their artworks by concentrating on what the historian Alexander Sturgis has called the 'memorably perceived phase' of motion – that is, 'when the direction of a movement changes'. You do not, observes Sturgis, illustrate a pendulum's swing halfway through, when it is pointing downwards; you illustrate the instant at which it begins reversing. In a batting stroke, these 'memorably perceived' phases are the beginning and the end. A bat upraised, exuding possibility, was to become a recurrent motif in cricket art, thanks in large part to one of the figures in the foreground of 'A Cricket Match'.

Nicholas Wanostrocht was a polymath schoolmaster from Blackheath who rejoiced in music, languages, art, science and cricket. His nom de plume, Felix, was a nod to Virgil's Georgics: *Felix, qui potuit rerum cognoscere causas* ('Fortunate is he who is able to know the causes of things'). He invented the original batting glove; he invented the first bowling machine; above all, he invented the study of cricket technique. There had been tutors before him, but none so comprehensive and matter-of-factly ambitious: 'My attempt is merely to prove that we may treat the subject with the same courtesy as any other scientific or skilled inquiry, and not ascribe to bad luck all that happens to the chance-surrounded batsman.'

In his explorations, Felix had an unlikely collaborator: painter and sculptor George Frederic Watts, pre-Raphaelite master in the making, but then the teenage son of a friend. From Watts, Felix commissioned pencil sketches demonstrating different shots, which were published as a series of popular lithographs, then adapted for Wanostrocht's masterwork *Felix on the Bat* (1845). They remain strikingly informative. In 'Play', for example, the batsman takes his stance, looking over his left shoulder, knees slightly bent, bat on the ground, feet at ten-to-two. The images of action then concentrate on 'memorably perceived' phases. In 'The Cut', 'Leg Volley' and 'Leg Half-Volley', the legs are wide apart and the bat being flourished; in 'Forward', 'Home Block' and 'The Draw' the stroke has been carried to completion. The comparison Felix draws in the text is between a right-handed batsman and a left-handed fencer moving between defence and attack. But he doesn't just tell – thanks to Watts, he also demonstrates.

Felicitous: Watts' 'The Leg Volley' and 'The Cut'.

Watts' images had a remarkable afterlife, informing almost every depiction of cricket action for the rest of the nineteenth century: as talented an artist as John Corbet Anderson, for instance, simply mimicked them when he assembled 'Cricketing Postures' in 1860. And when George Beldam captured Victor Trumper in 'Jumping Out', how did he convey potential drama but by a bat flamboyantly flourished?

•

'A Cricket Match' and *Felix on the Bat* are fruits of a period of great, if chaotic, growth in cricket, thanks to a long peace, the ceaseless spread of industry, the growing reach of rail, and the expansion of education, literacy and the franchise. Cricket was so busy expanding, in fact, that it had no particular need to cohere, and came under three overlapping spheres of influence: that of the emergent counties like Sussex, Kent, Surrey and Nottinghamshire; that of amateur Marylebone, the country's most prestigious club; that of the professional All-England XI, the country's most illustrious team. The amateur was not yet quite the hegemon he became; the professional still enjoyed the stature of a semi-independent artisan; some cricketers, like Felix, flitted between categories. If anything, the great travelling troupe of the All-England XI predominated, thanks to the energy and avarice of its impresario William Clarke. The summit of the amateur and professional rivalry, the Gentlemen v Players match at Lord's, regularly reiterated professional superiority, being won by the amateurs only seven times in forty-six matches between 1831 and 1865.

Except that professional cricket was a house growingly divided. After Clarke was succeeded on his death by George Parr, the All-England XI found itself rivalled by defectors and epigones competing for the same fixtures. Amateur talent emanating from the public schools reinvigorated both the indolent MCC, which had traditionally abbreviated its season so members could head for the moors in August, and the counties, whose controllers craved gentility in the newly industrialised landscape. Above all there loomed the figure of Dr W. G. Grace, who would seek the privileges of amateurism and the profits of professionalism, and contrive, such were his gifts, to secure them both. By the late 1850s and early 1860s, as professional cricketers clambered over one another in search of new markets, a new technology, the steamship, abruptly placed them within reach. In October 1861, a dozen venturesome professionals led by H. H. Stephenson of the All-England XI and Surrey boarded the SS *Great Britain*, whose screw propulsion and iron hull had halved voyage time to Australia. And in the spirit of newness they first paused in the stableyard of the Anglesea Hotel in the Haymarket, put on their creams, blue waistbelts and bow ties, and posed for a photograph.

Pioneers on parade: Stephenson's 1861 Englishmen.

•

Twenty years since Fox Talbot's patent of the calotype and Louis Daguerre's launch of the daguerreotype, photography had been thoroughly popularised – and, some felt, utterly debauched. Like cricket, it strained to distinguish amateur from professional. Its amateur pioneers had been a tight circle of gentleman scientists, antiquarians and artists, who debated photographs as well as taking and exchanging them, especially whether it was the purpose of the medium 'to avoid awkward forms, and to correct the unpicturesque', or merely to capture the 'beautiful and unconscious pose'. Wet collodion had then brought photography within reach of professionals with rudimentary knowledge, in particular those who specialised in *cartes de visite*, a genre of small images on albumen paper pasted onto cards so stunningly popular that their vogue was called 'cardomania'. Queen Victoria and Prince Albert bestowed their patronage when Roger Fenton founded the Royal Photographic Society in January 1853, and commissioned from him a dozen private works; but their greater royal impact would be participating in *carte de visite* portrait albums that sold in hundreds of thousands, especially after Albert's death. The versatile Fenton, a barrister with sufficient artistic pretentions to train as a painter in Paris, would experience tugs both ways.

In March 1854, Britain slid into a murky, maladministered war in the Crimea, joining an allied force that besieged Sebastopol. Prime Minister Lord Aberdeen was in turn besieged by the columns of the *Times* correspondent William Howard Russell describing dreadful casualties and indicting incompetent leadership. Whether for profit, public spirit or both, Fenton turned on the war his mechanical and chemical eye. It was as yet a blinking eye. His horsedrawn wagon of apparatus and ten-second exposure times were unequal to the action; his collodion dried in the heat almost as soon as he spread it on the plate; his Victorian sensibilities precluded his photographing casualties. His 350 usable negatives were thus mainly landscapes and panoramas, portraits of commanders and vignettes of soldiers well behind the lines, plus one cameo of a brooding Russell. Yet, seemingly independent and unmediated, these foundational 'war photographs' were critically acclaimed as 'actualities'.

Returning home, Fenton embarked on six frenetic years photographing an astonishing range of subjects: landscapes and lightscapes, still lives and stately homes, archaeological artefacts and orientalist tableaux. Striving to be neither dilettante nor hack, he found himself increasingly out of sympathy with his old amateur colleagues, who opposed members having 'any connexion with photography as a commercial speculation', and out of step with the customs of professionals, whose proliferation had caused the price of photographs to plunge. When the organising committee for the 1862 International Exhibition decided to bump photography from its accustomed place among the arts to among the lowlier crafts, otherwise reserved for machinery, tools and instruments, Fenton gave up: as Stephenson's team toured Australia, he was in the process of selling his equipment and portfolio.

In the meantime, however, Fenton had started something else. During 1857, when he was otherwise busily documenting the Elgin Marbles, cathedrals in Ely, Peterborough, Lincoln and York, and the crags, ravines and valleys of North Wales, he paused on 25 July at Islington's Artillery Ground and took five similar pictures of the Royal Artillery Cricket Club playing Hunsdonbury Cricket Club: cricket's oldest surviving photographs. It's unclear why Fenton did so when in his whole career he took no more than a handful of photographs of activities that could be called recreational. The Artillery Ground, too, was well past its heyday a century earlier; it more closely resembled a village green, rimmed with mature trees. Perhaps, like those painters who had incorporated cricket in their landscapes, Fenton regarded the game as straightforwardly scenic; perhaps he simply knew some members of the Royal Artillery XI from the Crimea.

In any event, Fenton faced similar perplexities to those earlier illustrators: unable to freeze the action with his camera, he had to curtail it by request; unable to ford the boundary, he had to make the best of his distance. Some effort was made at simulating action: the batsman stooped over his blade; the fielders faced toward the centre. But the chief activity around this photograph would have been Fenton's: first coating the plate with emulsion in his portable darkroom, hurrying to insert it in the holder, exposing it for five to ten seconds, then hastening to process the negative in its silver bath before the emulsion dried, all the while trying not to inhale too much ether vapour from the collodion, and this on a summer's day to boot. For Fenton, then, cricket and the Crimea posed surprisingly similar challenges.

Nor, it had to be said, was being photographed other than an ordeal, which accounts in some degree for the solemnity of Victorian portraits. 'Many people have remarked to me that George Parr had rather a morose and sullen expression as judged from the portraits seen of him,' recalled teammate Richard Daft of his All-England XI captain:

But I can assure the reader that he had a much pleasanter expression in reality than that which he often assumed when standing to be photographed, especially in those portraits taken of him with the rest of the XI, on which occasions the long time it took to arrange our positions, and the length of time we had to remain perfectly motionless, was most trying on the nerves . . .

Black and white green: Cricket's oldest photograph.

The local photographer would generally appear on the scene when we were at breakfast at an hotel, and send the waiter to request an interview with Mr Parr to make arrangements for our photos to be taken later in the day.

'Mr Parr, the photographer's here,' the waiter would announce.

'What, again!' George would exclaim with a look of disgust as he would reluctantly leave the table.

Soon enough it would be an ordeal there was no avoiding, wherever in the world you were.

•

There is a regularly published but still remarkable sepia photograph of a stagecoach containing H. H. Stephenson's Englishmen pulling up in Melbourne's Bourke Street on Christmas Eve 1861. Taken by a local specialist in theatrical *cartes de visite*, William Davies, it shows the cricketers perched atop the vehicle, purportedly the largest in the colony, which seems to be bobbing in a sea of hatted heads. Onlookers seeking better vantages prop on steps, peer out windows, mass around a lamppost, and in one case perch atop a sign advertising pantomime at next door's Theatre Royal; from the facade, broken by Tuscan columns, blare the names CAFÉ DE PARIS and THE VESTIBULE.

In this very first image of English players in Australia, then, are discernible two distinctive characteristics of colonial cricket: giddying public enthusiasm and brash commercialism, for the Café and the Vestibule signify the premises of Spiers & Pond, the tour's sponsor. It could hardly have been further removed from Fenton's tranquil scene with its sylvan fringe, but nor, really, could the Antipodes.

faction, excluding as it did the Melbourne CC, the SCG Trustees, and also the players. But its members had, like those colonial politicians toying with a draft Australian constitution, serious federal ambitions – nothing less than 'the regulation of visits of English or other teams' and 'the regulation of visits of Australasian teams to England or elsewhere'. The council began positively with a vote, albeit by the narrowest possible margin, to turn his lordship's sterling into 160 oz (4.5 kg) of symbolic silver – the Sheffield Shield.

Like the Federal Council of Australasia that the colonies had conceived of in 1883, the Australasian Cricket Council's title was as grand as its actual powers were small. It controlled no grounds, had neither income nor reserves. Players abided its constituting a selection panel, but resented its appointment of a manager on their next two tours of England; it was the Melbourne CC and the SCG Trustees who organised the next two tours by English teams. What the council would do over eight fitful years was hint at how a federal structure might work, while the associations themselves took other internal steps, such as the promotion of local pennant competitions along 'electoral' lines – that is, with players drawn from within defined residential boundaries, fostering local rivalries and more equal competition. Trumper's comment that 'there is nothing like the democracy of a sports ground', then, had quite particular resonances – ironically, as we shall see in Chapter 8, it would be his playing generation who ended up resisting the last step in that process.

•

The Australian summers of 1894–95 and 1897–98, when local teams for the first time met visiting teams across the expanse of five Test matches, set new standards in scale and scope. The wholesome blending of colonial cricket could be interpreted as preluding states-men's efforts towards actual union: thus *The Bulletin*'s oft-quoted remark about Australian cricket success doing 'more to enhance the cause of Australian nationality than could be achieved by miles of erudite essays and impassioned appeal'. Never before, too, had so many people been able to follow cricket. If daily newspapers were slow to exploit the development of the dry plate and the halftone block, weeklies such as *The Australasian* and *Australian Town and Country Journal* were now thickly lined with photographs, line drawings and engravings, and accorded Test and Sheffield Shield matches lush visual coverage. The accent remained on event rather than action – the distant white-clad figures might have been a flea circus. But in crowd panoramas, regularly spread over double pages, the 'democracy of a sports ground' was thoroughly in evidence. Other things, too.

In a vast, thinly populated land, the thronging to a Test match was a remarkable phenomenon. What explained it? Not only the craving for success, some thought; the spectacle itself formed part of the allure. Cricket exerted an 'unmeasured power of attraction', thought a *Sydney Morning Herald* contributor: 'It is an abiding joy to the participants, and a picture of grace and skill to the spectator. All its surroundings are delightful to the eye, and refreshing to the brain. Its geometric precision and the flashing celerity of polished movement are blandly exhilarating, and, without any extra charge at all, every onlooker may be a critic. And he generally is.' Cricket was restrained, refined, civilised, civilising – a game, thought a leader writer in *The Australasian* after a Melbourne Test, to 'delight the eye of the artist':

What athletes in classic games and times could surpass in swiftness
and grace of movement, in skill of wrist and quickness of eye and
enduring pluck, the white-clad figures that make up the players
in a great cricket match? The movements of a famous bowler like
Richardson or Turner are in the highest degree picturesque; and
a fine batsman like Gregory, or Darling, or Brockwell resembles
a fencer with his bat for rapier meeting with quick-turning parry
and lunge the attack, now subtle, now furious, of the bowler.

To an artist perhaps, the vast crowd of spectators, silent and
vigilant, is as picturesque and almost as interesting as the play.
Nearly twenty thousand spectators watched the play on New Year's
Day, and the floor of green turf was literally framed in a mighty
curving slope of human faces. No other sport produces exactly the
sort of crowd which a great cricket match attracts. A race meeting
is a sort of picnic, flavoured with tiny and intermittent doses of
intense excitement – excitement packed into a few seconds – when
a race is being actually run. A football match is two hours of mere
tumult, but the crowd at a [Test] match like that which has just
taken place will sit patiently from twelve o'clock till six for four
days in succession. It is for the most part silent and grave-faced;
the interest is too intense for frivolity! Every eddying turn and
change in the game is watched with fixed vigilance, punctuated
by short, sharp, and businesslike expressions of approval . . .
The youths whose faces made a living frieze above the curving
pickets could not perhaps give the kings of England, but they
know with familiar knowledge the names of every Australian
player, and the records of all the Australian Elevens.

These were unusual appeals. It was a common complaint of
Australians in colonial times that their jubilant materialism had

rendered them philistines, indifferent to civilising indulgences. Thus Richard Twopeny: 'It cannot be understood too thoroughly that Australia is before everything a money-making place.' Thus J. A. Froude: 'They [Australians] aim at little except what money will buy; and to make money and buy enjoyment with it is the be-all and end-all of their existence.' Thus Francis Adams: 'To speak of "culture" and "society" in Australia, in the sense that one does of the greater European capitals, would be like speaking of the snakes of Iceland. Disinterested study is unknown in a country where every one is still in haste to gamble, grab land, or create a business.' But in cricket, some were now arguing, lay a form of aesthetic and intellectual redemption – it was the stylish game, the cerebral game, where a subtle critic might discern worlds by a look.

•

This change also reflected the impress of English ideas, and the influence of English personalities. By the late Victorian age, the English regarded their summer game, diffused by mass transportation and promoted by the print media, with deep satisfaction. Test matches were less frequent but more meaningful; the County Championship was firmly established. Unlike rugby, cricket had not fissured along class and regional lines; unlike football, it retained an inviolable amateur primacy, the professional XIs having long disbanded. There was also a growing corpus of popular literature. Guides and collections abounded, the majority of them cheap, but some expensive and lavishly illustrated with lithographs, woodcuts and portrait photographs such as the first edition of *The Badminton Book of Cricket* (1888), tenth and most prestigious in the Duke of Beaufort's *Badminton Library of Sports and Pastimes*. Despite his deeming writing 'not a recreation I care for', Grace's *Cricket* (1891) weighed in at 500 pages, bulked up with advices such as 'do not go into the field with a cigarette or pipe in your mouth'; his old rival Billy Murdoch's *Cricket* (1894), part of 'The Oval' series, extended to a more modest ninety-five pages. Most splendid was Charles Alcock's *Famous Cricketers and Cricket Grounds* (1895), published in eighteen instalments by the *News of the World*: 272 full-page portraits of 110 amateurs, 105 professionals, sixteen Australians, nineteen teams, three administrators and two umpires, some at the wicket, some posed as if waiting to be painted while gazing wistfully into the middle distance. Grace took precedence, the ageless guru, beard still youthfully dark. The assemblage was also flecked with glamour, two figures standing out.

Resembling a young Byron was Oxford University's Charles Burgess Fry. By 1895, he was the epitome of the all-round Englishman, already heavy with academic and athletic laurels: a first-class classicist, a triple captain in cricket, football and athletics. He was playing amateur football for Corinthians, amateur rugby for Barbarians. He had equalled the world long-jump record. He had also leapt into the pages of *Vanity Fair* as a subject, 'Spy' stressing the noble profile of the 'dark blue hero', and into the pages of *Isis*, *Badminton* and *New Review* as a writer, where he espoused reliably high-minded opinions ('a strong leaven of amateurism is absolutely necessary for the good of the game').

The other, dark features accentuated by his billowing silk shirt, was the figure from whom Fry's name would become inseparable: Cambridge's Kumar Shri Ranjitsinhji. 'Kumar Shri,' Alcock added helpfully, 'it may be useful to add signifies Prince.' Up to a point: Ranji was actually a village farmer's son adopted as an heir by the Jam Saheb of a tiny Indian statelet, Nawanagar, as a precaution

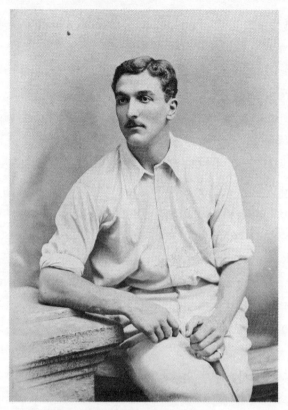

Cricket magnifico: C. B. Fry.

against that potentate's inability to father an heir of his own. That status had been revoked with the arrival of an heir four years later, and Ranji had arrived in England uncertain of his future. Cricket had embraced him, and Fry too, when Ranji whisked him to the mid-wicket boundary in a game at Hove. 'To me,' Fry recalled, 'the stroke was a revelation of an entirely new technique only possible to a player with a quickness of eye, a nicety of poise, a surety of foot and a control of hand far superior to the best English practice.'

Fry was intrigued by technique. His own, he thought disapprovingly, was limited and mechanical, set into ruts by coaching at Repton from a master who 'offered a few general sarcasms' and a 'fat old professional' who knew 'just exactly nothing about the art of batsmanship'.

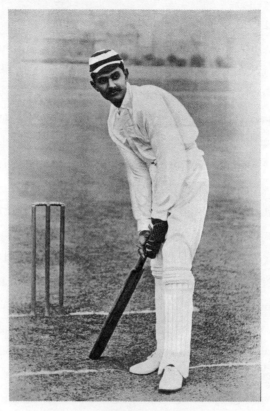

His serene majesty: Ranjitsinhji.

Fry had been raised, for example, to regard the leg side as positively vulgar: 'If one hit a ball in an unexpected direction to the on-side, intentionally or otherwise, one apologised to the bowler . . . The opposing captain never by any chance put a fieldsman there; he expected you to drive on the off-side like a gentleman, even if his bowlers presented stuff which . . . one could turn into long-hops to leg.' When they teamed up with Sussex the following season, Fry studied Ranji as intently as a naturalist alighting on a new species. Noting Ranji's supple wrists, prehensile fingers and quicksilver reflexes, he deemed himself inferior in every respect, and strove to improve.

The moment was ripe. Grace was approaching fifty, his star quietly waning. Ranji's 1896 debut for England, an unbeaten 154 against

Australia at Old Trafford, established him as cricket's coming man. 'Grace has nothing to teach him as a batsman,' pronounced the *Manchester Guardian*. 'And none of the men of renown of thirty years ago could have exhibited a more thorough mastery of every point of the game.' And although Ranji remained showily deferential to the cricketer he simply called 'The Champion', his style of batting clearly represented an exquisite advance. Slim, lithe and athletic, his backswing a twirl, his batspeed a flash, his leg glance a signature, he revealed batting possibilities never previously divined. The pace of a bowler could be turned against them by an artfully angled bat; the traditional concentration of fielders to the off side could accordingly be foiled. These were subversive, even revolutionary ideas: in a sense Ranji's difference was licensed by his exotic origins, even as misgivings about these were allayed by his overt imperialism. 'It has always been, and will always be, my endeavour in my humble way to bring about real brotherly love between the two nations,' he said at the Cambridge banquet in his honour at the end of that season. 'From the very beginning I have been connected with the English people, and have a great liking and enthusiasm for their high social and intellectual qualities.'

The Englishman to whom he most closely connected was Fry, who when they batted together was regarded as providing a kind of rational, occidental counterpart to Ranji's venturesome oriental speculations. In common they had improvidence – living effortlessly, as amateurs were expected to, was extraordinarily hard work. Ranji had at least an erratic stipend and a supply of oriental baubles and regalia; once a modest Oxford scholarship ceased, Fry had no income to speak of. Cricket, fortunately, was holding forth new possibilities. Ranji was invited to monetise his fame by producing a cricket guide; Fry, lumbered with a teaching job at Charterhouse that he cordially despised, was the perfect amanuensis. *The Jubilee*

*Book of Cricket* (1897), dedicated 'by her Gracious Permission, to Her Majesty the Queen-Empress', was a detailed *tour d'horizon* of the English game, and also a manifesto for amateur supremacy. Heaven forfend that cricket should emulate football's trend towards professional control: 'Facts show that the majority of elevens composed entirely or even principally of professionals do not succeed . . . There is no doubt that if the high standard of what may be called "sportsmanship" is to be maintained, amateurs must continue to form a fair proportion of the entire body of first-class cricketers.'

The *Jubilee Book* was an immediate craze, establishing Ranji and Fry as to cricket what Walter Pater and John Ruskin were to literature and art – setters of standards, arbiters of beauty. It traded first of all on Ranji's eastern singularity but was enriched by the ring of Fry's classical learning, in praise for The Champion ('He [Grace] turned the one-stringed instrument into a many-chorded lyre, and, in addition, he made his execution equal to his invention') and for 'the heroic' more generally ('I can imagine Agamemnon, Achilles and their peers not unbecomingly engaged in a cricket-match'). Helped by constant publicity from the collaborators' piling up 22 000 first-class runs at an average of more than 60, royalties over the next five years exceeded £7000.

In the year of the *Jubilee Book*, Ranji also paid his first visit to Australia as a member of Drewy Stoddart's English team, making 1154 runs in a dozen first-class matches, and proving so popular that colonial governments waived their taxes on coloured persons. 'The prospect of meeting the princely author of *The Jubilee Book of Cricket*, and of seeing a dark prince batting and bowling like any other cricketer, may . . . account for the vast number of ladies present at the intercolonial cricket match on the new grounds at Woolloongabba,' reported *The Queenslander*. 'All eyes were centred on Prince Ranjitsinhji; little boys followed him about, little girls longed to do so, too.' Watching crowds outside his office at *The Australasian* awaiting telegraphed updates of the cricket scores caused 'Woomera' to wonder at his fellow citizens' priorities:

Why do they come with one accord,
Together in one place?
Why do they gaze upon that board,
Whilst joy illumes each face?
Why do the youngsters babble so?
Why do the old men shout?
Is federation carried? No;
But Ranjitsinhji's out.

Colonial audiences were in thrall to Ranji's every stroke, almost his every word – for his reports in the *Australian Review of Reviews* were voluminous, sometimes provocative. One view that met widespread approval was of a junior batsman representing New South Wales against the tourists. 'He created a very favourable impression on me from the way he was shaping at the wickets,' reported Ranji. 'He seemed to be all there, and the confidence with which he played the bowling, although it was for a very short time, makes me firmly believe that he will be a very great batsman in this country, and at no very distant date. Indeed, I have seen very few beginners play the ball so well, and show the same excellent style.' This was a remarkably fulsome prophecy for a batsman who made 5 and 0 in the match. Yet Ranji was far from the first to so respond to Victor Trumper.

•

The story of the emergence of every sporting champion is an invitation to speculate on *that* moment when special qualities proclaimed themselves. In the case of Trumper, this is more than usually difficult. The great early scores are not really there. A chronicle of his junior career at Crown Street School and Carlton CC published in 2015 by the assiduous historian Alf James divulged no legacy of stupendous records. But what was unmistakably present, contemporaries insisted, was a 'look', first discerned by his father during their dawn practices: 'Every day I would note some degree of improvement in his skill with the bat and in his style of play, which needless to say was a source of much gratification for me.' The effect was enhanced by his willowy figure. He was 'short, spare, narrow-shouldered', inspiring nobody 'with the idea of athleticism in any direction'. He was the smallest boy in a line drawing of the Crown Street team; he was an incongruously slim youth in shorts among Carlton's hardy, hirsute men, who numbered among them the legendary Charles Bannerman, Test cricket's first century maker. But put a bat in his hands and he seemed to have intuited batting from first principles.

How and why did Trumper stand out so in the colonial cricket of the 1890s? The game was only just being regularised. Techniques remained homespun. Batting was unenterprising. Distances precluded more than half a dozen Sheffield Shield fixtures per season, each played to a finish, which made for long phases of austerity. If a bowler pursued the prevalent 'off theory' – a line wide of off stump to a packed off-side field – a batsman could in theory forswear strokes indefinitely. Trumper, it is clear, never played this way. Twenty years after events, a contemporary recalled Bannerman's early efforts to train Trumper to no avail: 'For a time all went well, but young Trumper, having mastered the defensive tactics of the game, began to do a little original work in the way of the most daring strokes.

In vain Bannerman called out, "Leave it alone, Vic; that wasn't a ball to go at.'" It seems to have been decided quite early, in fact, that Trumper's cricket called simply for encouragement. What he acquired rather than coaches were advocates.

With the thinness of club facilities in Sydney, the practice pitches at the Randwick end of the SCG were heavily used, and Trumper exposed to an ever wider circle. Tom Garrett, the captain of New South Wales in the Sheffield Shield, was a first important patron, ensuring that there was never question of the youngster's availability for cricket by bringing him into his public-service office, the registry of probates and curator of intestate estates. He also spread word by introducing Trumper to other knowledgeable judges as 'the most promising boy in the world', including the captain of the Test team, Jack Blackham. After studying a few strokes, Blackham apparently agreed. 'My word, Tom,' he said. 'Isn't he like Charles Bannerman?'

When the advent of electoral cricket in Sydney delivered Trumper to Paddington CC, he impressed himself on two other influential judges, then serving as that club's delegates to the NSWCA. One was John Corbett Davis, Sydney's encyclopedist of sports journalism, who at *The Referee* wrote cricket as 'Not Out' and rugby as 'The Cynic', and also published the *Australian Cricket Annual*. A trim, dapper man always attired in dark blue, affecting a bowler hat and *pince-nez*, he was a fixture at the SCG nets whomever was practising. Davis was instantly agog: 'Everyone soon knew the phenomenal boy who batted and bowled and fielded, without a word, without an atom of self-consciousness, as though he were born an international player . . . It was a tonic to spend ten minutes watching him play.' It was a tonic for which Davis never lost the taste – over the next fifty years, nobody would write more about Trumper.

The other Paddington clubmate was Monty Noble, an alumnus

of Crown Street four and a half years Trumper's senior. He was handsome, manly, a fine all-round cricketer, and a sportsman dense with moral fibre: 'Cricket teaches you to be clean. The exercise and environment promote clean thoughts. It discountenances boastfulness, shady tricks, and unhealthy practices, and sets high value on quiet demeanour, gentlemanly conduct and modesty.' One sight of Trumper was sufficient for Noble to come away convinced that he was beyond instruction: 'You could talk to him, and coach him. He would listen carefully, respect your advice and opinions and, leaving you, would forget all you had told him, play as he wanted to play.'

Here, then, was an early example of that faith, still common among athletes, fans, coaches, commentators, talent scouts and player agents alike, that the best are set apart, not only quantifiably, but somehow by how they look, or how they move, or how they prepare – a quality more compelling for being sometimes beyond description. In Trumper's case, the basis of this general conviction can never truly be known. There remained no practical means of capturing and representing 'action': the only surviving photograph of Garrett bowling shows him, aged seventy-nine, by then the very last survivor of the very first Test, delivering the first ball of a match at the SCG in February 1938 to mark the sesquicentenary of white settlement in Australia, wearing dark trousers, a waistcoat and the hat he removed not even at mealtimes. What does endure is the utmost confidence of the claims for him. In their inference that a player could be distinguished by 'style', they reflect a step in the game's aesthetic evolution, a ramifying of Ranji's impact on entranced crowds.

This 'style' of Trumper's, of course, had first to be seen. And seeing, as the nineteenth century ended, required being in the right place at the right time. In his late teens, Trumper began piling up runs for Paddington, especially at its home ground, Hampden

Mentor: the sole surviving 'action' photograph of Tom Garrett.

Park. For New South Wales, too, he compiled bulging double hundreds against two weak opponents, Tasmania and New Zealand, at the SCG. But in fourteen other first-class matches over four years, Trumper made only three half-centuries, and eighteen scores under 20. When boosters championed Trumper's inclusion in the Australian team to tour England in 1899, they encountered what Noble admitted was entirely legitimate scepticism:

> Most of the opposition to his inclusion came from Victoria and Adelaide, for, they said, and with plenty of justification: 'We have good young cricketers with records to prove their ability. And, in any case, we just haven't *seen* Trumper.' That was just what we had been telling them. They had not *seen* him; 'but once you do,' we declared, 'there will be no doubt in your minds.' [my italics]

During the first of three trial matches for the team, in Sydney, Davis cornered its manager, Major Ben Wardill, and submitted him to a passionate advocacy. One glimpse of Trumper, Davis insisted, was all it would take. He felt Wardill's scepticism harden: 'The Major was a most genial man, and I remember as we parted he remarked, "You Sydney people are married to Trumper. What has he done to justify it?" To that I answered, "Good-bye, Major. If you had him in Melbourne you'd soon understand it."' But Trumper did nothing out of the ordinary in the first two of the games, and went unnamed in the thirteen-member squad.

Deliverance came at the eleventh hour. In the last trial match, at Adelaide Oval, the day after which the team was due to depart, Trumper made 75. It must have been very good. It was no small thing for the Australians to welcome an additional member, for it diluted their profit pool. But the selectors reconvened and decided to expand their squad with a fourteenth member doubling as an assistant manager, on a fixed stipend rather than a full share. As Noble recalled it:

> Major Wardill, the manager, came to me towards the end of
> the third trial match in Adelaide and said: 'Do you want Victor
> Trumper to go to England?'
> 'Rather,' I replied.
> 'Well,' he said, 'you can go and tell him that he is selected.'
> I could hardly believe my ears.

But his colleagues, as implored, had believed their eyes.

•

This 1899 tour, the first in England to feature as many as five Tests, was unusually freighted with expectations. With the second Federation referendum scheduled to seek public endorsement while the team was away, Joe Darling's men were a kind of aspirational symbol: the pithy suffrage advocate Rose Scott, in fact, had derided the whole federalist campaign a 'glorified cricket match'. A few weeks prior to departure, the core of the team attended a Sydney Town Hall benefit concert for Trumper's erstwhile club teammate Charles Bannerman, where they were addressed by Edmund Barton and George Reid, long-time political rivals recently reconciled in the federal cause, who also doubled as vice-presidents of the NSWCA. It was the politicians being honoured by the presence of the cricketers rather than the other way around, thought a correspondent of *The Australasian*: 'The sight of those manly heroes in ordinary garb, sitting so modestly in the body of the hall, as if hardly conscious of the honour they were conferring upon the rulers of the coming Australian nation, was an intoxicating sight, calculated to turn the soberest head.' Reid and Barton duly laid on the blandishments:

> The remarks which followed were a charming blend of Federation and cricket. Mr. Reid implored the departing Eleven not to think, as was the custom 20 years ago, that all the people in the other colonies were rogues and swindlers. He said – with tears in his eyes – that he knew the Victorians were honest men; he had said so before, and he now said it again.
>
> Mr. Barton called on the Eleven to remain true to the nation which they would belong to on their return. If defeated they were to bear defeat nobly, and if victorious to bear it modestly. In any case, the hearts of Federated Australians would beat as one over

the issue. Mr. Barton concluded by hoping that in conduct, manners, and morals the Eleven would prove themselves worthy of the great Australian nation.

Joe Darling stepped forward, with his hand upon his heart, and declared that that should be their only endeavour.

The irony is that in the organising of their tour, Darling and his comrades were undertaking what was still a private speculation. Contemptuous of the colonial associations' pretensions to governing the game, they had partnered with the Melbourne CC, whose advance on the tour's proceeds enabled them again to visit England as cricket's best-compensated amateurs. This tolled the knell on the Australasian Cricket Council, shortly wound up with all of £10 in the bank, survived by a single idea that the players appropriated – a recent suggestion, by South Australian council member Mostyn Evan, that the Australian team settle on a uniform set of colours. Rather than adopt the red, white and blue Melbourne raiment favoured by the 1886 team, Darling's team had blazers tailored and boaters banded in Evan's idea of green and gold; they hoisted a green-and-gold standard from the flagpole above their London base, the Inns of Court Hotel in High Holborn; they presented a green-and-gold bouquet to the contralto Ada Crossley when she performed for them in Eastbourne. With an allusion to the tour's likely profitability, the *West Australian* reported: 'The colours of the Australian team are sage green with gold-braided edge. More gold than green about the wearers, though.'

Whether on proto-national or personal account, the team played like men on a mission, determined to outlast where they could not outplay. They won the only Test decided; the rest they dourly drew, thankful that Tests in England lasted only three days. All the while they kept a watchful eye on the bottom line. During the Test at Manchester, the local county secretary half-jokingly offered Ben Wardill £250 if Darling would declare the innings closed and make a game of it. 'Make it £500 and we'll consider it,' Darling replied. Still nursing a soupçon of irritation about the Australians' professional amateurism, the English lapsed occasionally into mockery. After Noble dawdled eight hours over 60 not out and 89 at Old Trafford, an anonymous donor posted him a leather medal inscribed in honour of his landmark of '1000 runs in 1000 years'. When Darling took three hours over 39 at Lord's, the crowd whistled 'We Won't Get Home Till Morning' and the 'Dead March' from *Saul*. As a mute protest against the visitors' professional amateurism, the *Daily Mail* and *Daily Telegraph* withheld the 'Mr' from before their names on scoreboards.

Complaints about Australian obstinacy, however, also had to be qualified by reference to Trumper. For Trumper took chances, lots of chances – sometimes too many. Equally, it emerged, he could scatter and demoralise an attack in half an hour. In the decisive Test at Lord's, Trumper made an unbeaten 135 after Australia had slipped to three for 59 in pursuit of 206. Five weeks later his undefeated triple century against Sussex at Hove – 380 minutes, thirty-six boundaries – was the first by an Australian in England. Only the sternly safe Noble and Darling scored more runs on the tour, and Noble took satisfaction in Darling's becoming a Trumperphile just as ardent. 'What do I think of him?' Darling responded when Noble asked him one day. 'I thought I could bat!'

It was not only for his batting that teammates promoted Trumper to a full profit share – the gesture was also a personal tribute. Eight months of more or less constant travel and play revealed natures reliably. 'The Kid', as comrades called him, became a team favourite – polite, kind, ingenuous. Jack Worrall: 'A more obliging or sweet-tempered boy never lived. Nothing was a trouble to him: everything was a pleasure, and he endeared himself to all of us by his disposition alone.' Frank Iredale: 'He had one of those natures which called to you, and in whose presence you felt it was good to live.' Clem Hill: 'Trumper was a most loving and unassuming champion . . . No batsman ever played more for his side.' Hugh Trumble: 'What an inspiration he was!' Noble, always Noble, with tales to be endlessly repeated: 'Coming out of the London Coliseum one cold wet night he saw a boy shivering in a doorway selling music. Victor broke away from the rest of us, spoke to the lad, bought the whole of his stock-in-trade and sent the youngster home happy.' The captain? One of his eight sons he would christen Victor.

•

For his own part in 1899, Trumper bequeathed no memoirs, letters or diaries. The fragmentary actualities that survive do so almost by accident. Since the opening of the new Lord's pavilion a decade earlier, for example, occupants of the visitors' dressing-room on the second floor had taken to carving their initials in the balcony. The Australians joined in. There is a solemnly precise 'M. A. Noble', a cheerfully informal 'Eva' and 'Lightning' – the nicknames of Hugh Trumble and Charlie McLeod respectively. On the fourth brick from right in what is now a members' bar, one still finds the etched abbreviation 'VT99'. There is no pecking order here: nearest by his is the name 'E. Reeves', who made 0 not out and did not bowl representing London Playing Fields against MCC four years later.

A few weeks after Trumper's triple century, Darling recalled, he opened his bag and saw a bat he did not recognise. It was the bat, a 'W.G.G.' made in Birmingham by W. G. Grenville, that Trumper had used at Hove, slipped in surreptitiously with the polite dedication: 'To Joe Darling with/V. Trumper's compliments/300 not out v Sussex/29/7/99'. It reposes today behind glass at Melbourne's National Sports Museum, fresh as the day it was last used, reflecting the care and honour with which Australia's captain treated it, with a family rededication: 'To Victor/From/Father/25/3/35/Joe Darling'.

The outline of the mechanical means by which memories would be laid down was also just visible. In the museum of the Melbourne CC are more than 1000 photographs taken by Frank Laver, who shared a cabin with Trumper and Noble aboard the *Ormuz* at the outset of the journey – the beginning of a friendship that would profoundly influence Australian cricket history. About 100 photographs survive from this trip, when Laver was simply a twenty-nine-year-old all-rounder from Castlemaine and 'inveterate snapshotter'. In the swirl of figures, only the cricketers have remained identifiable, the names of their hosts, guests, friends and acquaintances lost to time.

Laver's teammates were actually not overfond of photography. During the 1897–98 series against England, Darling and Clem Hill had been persuaded to pose for photographs while not out overnight, then been dismissed soon after play resumed, nourishing a superstitious aversion to cameras. Laver, however, was one of their own number. He mixed easily, and his images as a result are disarmingly candid. Nobody mugs. There are no silly poses or uneasy rictuses. Instead players breakfast in their pyjamas, cavort in a swimming pool, skip rope and play deck games on board ship, savour beauty spots and historic sites. Trumper is captured as a tourist in Portsmouth, on the deck of HMS *Victory* near where Nelson fell – visiting colonial, loyal Britisher.

Darling's Australians even had a brush with the newest of all technologies. Playing out their tour after the Fifth Test, they stopped at Cheltenham to play Gloucestershire, lost the toss and filed onto the College Ground on a bright, sunny day in front of a full house. We know this because we can see it, in the oldest surviving film footage of Australian cricketers.

The emergent motion-picture industry had been stalking cricket a while. On their visit to Australia eighteen months earlier, the magnetic Ranji and his teammate Tom Hayward had played 'some imaginary cricket for the special benefit of the cinematograph' in the nets at the SCG, footage shown in England with the sound effect of bat on ball synchronised. Later that same year a camera was set up in the assistant secretary's garden at Lord's so that the teams in the Gentlemen v Players match, made special by the coincidence of W. G. Grace's fiftieth birthday, could sweep past in smoothly curved lines – vanishing from view, Grace ceremoniously doffs his cap.

The Australians exhibited a variety of responses to British Mutoscope's presence. Trumper even appears slightly nonplussed, walking on with Darling, burly Ernie Jones and diminutive Syd Gregory, pausing to exchange a word with his skipper, back turned shyly – seemingly a characteristic attitude. As Trumper moves out of frame, Darling pauses to look at the cameraman before stagily beckoning his men on. Iredale points cheerfully towards the device. Wardill appears for a last-minute conference. Before the twenty-five-second sequence ends, Laver, Noble, Jim Kelly and Hugh Trumble have also been glimpsed. It is raw footage, without intertitles, credits or, of course, soundtrack. It's unclear whether it was even shown.

Examining such artefacts today, one is struck mainly by the miracle of their survival, so much else having perished between times. Apparently there was distant film footage of the Fifth Test at The

Oval, including of Ranji and Darling – a 'marvellous reproduction of the principal events in connection with the test matches played in the old country' according to an *Advertiser* report of attractions at Adelaide's Theatre Royal at Christmas 1899. Along with ninety-five per cent of the moving picture film stock shot before the World War I, it is long gone. Yet such fragments of fragments as do endure testify to a deeply felt impulse to leave a trace, out of a sense of participating in deeds of lasting significance. They are the harbinger of a recording century to come, in which the necessary means and media would be increasingly within everyday reach, and Victor Trumper would provide one of cricket's most indelible motifs.

# 3

# 'THE FIRST BATSMAN OF HIS TIME'

'I am not above suspicion in my use of words
when it comes to writing of Trumper.'
– NEVILLE CARDUS, *The Summer Game* (1929)

After the Fifth Test of Australia's series with England in 1902, London's *Daily Express* came up with a charitable notion. The *Express* would seek the bats of famous cricketers from home and abroad, England and Australia, and auction them for the benefit of England's Cricketers' Fund Friendly Society, a charity for broken-down old pros on hard times. Items were widely forthcoming, with an implement volunteered by W. G. Grace taking pride of place.

Except that the bat that everyone wanted belonged to the Australian Victor Trumper: at £42, it was sold at thrice the price of the next most valuable, that of the redoubtable Ranjitsinhji. Although Gilbert Jessop had just made a record-breaking seventy-five-minute century at The Oval, his bat fetched just £8.

Pride was at stake. A flurry of telegrams and telephone calls were necessary to flush out an anonymous, face-saving £50 bid for the bat of The Champion. Unaware of the backstage machinations, the Antipodean press thought the tribute sufficient. 'There is peculiar source of satisfaction for Australians in the fact that Trumper's piece of willow was so eagerly sought after,' reported the *Wellington Times*. 'It is a recognition of his magnificent prowess in the cricket field, and that he is held so near the purchasing power of Dr. Grace, the still famous hero of nearly half a century's cricket, speaks volumes.' Grace was, in any event, a hero of yesteryear. As *Cricket of Today* stated quite simply, 1902 had stamped Trumper 'as unquestionably the first batsman of his time'.

Even in Scotland: *Edinburgh Evening News*, 2 August 1902.

That made him, effectively, the first *Australian* of his time – the first to be the best in the world at *anything*. His only true rival was Dame Nellie Melba, appearing that summer in *Rigoletto* at Covent Garden. But Melba had spent sixteen years abroad – in a pursuit at which Australians measured themselves, Trumper went forth and returned as ascertainably the best. Australia, moreover, had been a nation barely a year and a half, and even then in name rather than substance: it had no anthem of its own, no coinage, official flag or heraldry; it deferred to British legislation and vice-regal authority; it had no power to declare war or peace, conclude treaties or be represented diplomatically. Trumper, then, also incarnated Australian possibilities.

In 1899, the tour's backdrop had been Federation; in 1902, it was coronation, counting in some respects for more, as Australians' imperial loyalty was rather stronger than their incipient nationalism. Henry Lawson urged his countrymen to combine the two in 'From the Bush' (1902): 'Hold up your heads in London/Tread firm in London streets!/We come from where the strong heart/Of all Australia beats.' Some took him up on the idea. Prominent expatriates formed London's Austral Club in the Bayswater drawing room of the *Daily Chronicle*'s chief foreign correspondent, Sydney-born Martin Donohue – members included actor Oscar Asche, composer George Clutsam, artists Arthur Streeton and John Longstaff, and novelists Rosa Praed and Mary Gaunt. They had much success to toast: the Australian rifle team won the Kolapore Cup at Bisley; Manly's Fred Lane swam 100 yards (91 metres) in less than a minute at Leicester. But none quickened hearts like the cricketers.

Trumper would change the way the English saw Australians too. Darling's team arrived with baggage, regarded as canny opponents but still not quite on social or cultural par. In *The Lighter Side of Cricket* (1901), Captain Philip Trevor, an army officer who wrote shrewdly as 'Dux' for *The Sportsman*, was politely scathing about Australian batsmen – 'difficult . . . to get out', but from whose 'masterly inactivity' the English had 'absolutely nothing to learn'. 'They have great patience and great stamina, and in their own country, when a match is played to a finish, even if it lasts for a fortnight, these qualities stand them in good stead,' wrote Trevor. 'But in England we manage matters differently, and the object of every sportsman is to inflict rather than avoid defeat.' Not to put too fine a point on it, Trevor thought the Australians, tenacity and defiance rooted in gate-money mindedness, had generally been bad for the game: 'The Australians have reduced to a fine art the practice of making the English three-day match last its full three days, and in doing so they have dealt a severe blow to the best interests of English cricket.'

Interestingly, Trevor's opinions were not based on his actually having seen the Australians play in 1899 – he had been on duty in South Africa. They reflected, rather, opinion stubbornly hard to shift. Which makes what followed all the more remarkable – here would be a first rehearsal of the idea, now deeply rooted in both countries, that Australian cricketers are innately aggressive, and set a tempo for the English to follow. In 1902, then, Victor Trumper was not simply playing cricket for his country; he was helping to invent it.

•

Trumper and 1902 elide in cricket history in the same way as Grace and 1895, Denis Compton and 1947, Viv Richards and 1976, Ian Botham and 1981 – great players in their purest avatars. Yet Trumper's golden summer also differs from these. It can be measured not just by the excellence of Trumper, but by the mediocrity

of others. *Wisden*'s first-class averages present the case straightforwardly: in 1902 just six batsmen made 1000 runs at an average in
excess of 40, while twenty-seven bowlers took at least fifty wickets at less than 20. From this Trumper's record stands out as if in
copperplate: 2570 first-class runs with eleven hundreds, both records
by a visitor, at an average of 48.49 uninflated by a single not out.
Only Arthur Shrewsbury, the indefatigable Nottinghamshire professional, slightly headed Trumper in the averages, with half as many
runs and seven not-outs; only Bobby Abel, Surrey's eternal favourite, came near him for runs, with 2229 in eleven more innings.

The reason was rain, not so much the amount, actually slightly
below average, as the sheer frequency. Rainy days in May, as the
Australians arrived, were a third greater than usual. June, July and
August were nearly as bad. When it wasn't raining, it looked about
to rain, the worst possible conditions for batting: lots of disrup-
tions, few outright washouts. On the era's uncovered pitches, the
Australians endured some grim days: England bowled them out for
36 at Edgbaston, Yorkshire for 23 at Bramall Lane. But all the while,
the normally staid *Wisden* observed, Trumper seemed to be *playing
another game*:

> Trumper stood alone among the batsmen of the season, not only
> far surpassing his own colleagues, but also putting into the shade
> everyone who played for England ... Having regards to its many
> wet days and soft wickets, it is safe to say that no-one – not even
> Ranjitsinhji – has been at once so brilliant and so consistent since
> W. G. Grace was at his best. Trumper seemed independent of the
> varying conditions, being able to play just as dazzling a game after
> a night's rain as when the wickets were hard and true. All bowling
> came alike to him and on many occasions, notably in the Test

matches at Sheffield and Manchester and the first of the two games
with MCC at Lord's, he reduced our best bowlers for the time
being to the level of the village green.

The year 1902 was on its way to becoming the gateway myth of the
Trumper legend, with the advantage of being anchored in reality – in
conditions as alien to him as could be, a twenty-four-year-old from
Sydney established himself as batting's foremost exponent. Yet this
also raises fundamental questions. *How* did Trumper bat? What
did he *look like*? He was clearly an improved version of the gifted
stripling who had visited three years earlier, but in what respects
had he advanced? And these questions are disconcertingly difficult
to answer. 'Pages might be written about Trumper's batting without exhausting the subject,' *Wisden* claimed – and they were. But
to revisit the contemporaneous reportage of the tour is to be disappointed. Cricket was still at the stage where it was reported rather
than genuinely written; newspaper journalism was about the con-
veyance of information rather than of impression. To search for
images from 1902 is likewise to leave dismayed. There was not even
Frank Laver on this tour to capture the Australians backstage, as
it were. Still as far off as ever, action remained largely the domain
of newspaper sketchers – versatile men like Frank Gillett, Ernest
Prater and S. T. Dadd who might be asked for a line drawing of a
regal occasion one day, to recreate the drama of a shipwreck the next.
The *Daily Graphic*, for example, had Gillett at each day of the summer's big games, and his facile pen provided the nearest thing to a
surviving visual record of Trumper's startling century in the first session of the Fourth Test at Old Trafford.

A few tentative conclusions can be drawn. Trumper was a
rapid scorer – his runs per minute, then the standard measure, are

TRUMPER AND DUFF DO WHAT THEY LIKE FOR THE FIRST HOUR AND A QUARTER

R.A.DUFF

A NEAR THING FOR TRUMPER

FRED TATE

LILLEY CATCHES DUFF

BRAUND'S SAD MISTAKE

FRANK GILLETT. MANCHESTER.

Action penmanship: Day one at Old Trafford.

appreciably faster than any other Australian's. Trumper was a versatile strokemaker – no writer stresses a particular strength or signature stroke. His batting was unconstrained by circumstance, such as state of game, quality of bowling, placement of field, and he seems to have been loath to play defensively *at all*. 'It is necessary for most batsmen to play the game for a few overs before unfolding their strokes,' wrote Noble. 'Not so with Victor.' And these factors challenged the stereotypes. England, where the flower of cricket was amateur, freed from the dull cares of earning a living, had always been the home of pedigree batsmanship; lacking gentlemanly polish and refinement, Australia had conventionally been seen as the forge of a grim cricket efficiency. Yet Trumper at the crease did not suggest preoccupation with the gate money of the day, or his share of spoils at tour's end. Writing in *The Strand* magazine in 1902, C. B. Fry, cricket's *arbiter elegantiae*, struggled to incorporate Trumper's nationality into an appreciation: 'Trumper appears to unite in his person the utilitarian virtues of Australia with the artistic virtues of the old country; or, perhaps, it is fair to say he is more like a very good English batsman than a very good Australian.' By batting like the very carefree amateurs that Australians had always purported to be, and which a certain English school had held they were not, he became a freak of cricket nature.

One of the most perceptive appreciations of Trumper, composed with the zeal of the convert, came from the pen of the aforementioned Trevor, who described how difficult it was 'to follow exactly what he [Trumper] was doing with his bat':

> I will try to substantiate that statement at the risk of being prosaic. Extend the bowling-crease to the boundary on both sides of the ground; then bowl to Trumper an ordinary, medium-paced, good-length ball. Trumper could hit that ball to any spot on the boundary in front of that extended white line ... You would watch these successful strokes, and you could not tell accurately as the bat came onto the ball the exact direction in which the batsman intended the ball to go. Trumper knew it himself almost to the 'minute of the degree'. His knowledge, indeed, of batting angles was too exact for the ordinary eye to follow.

I am still blessed with good ordinary eyesight. I can read figures and names on hoardings in a way that ought to make advertisers feel that they have not spent their money in vain. The bull's eye at Bisley 1000 yards [914 metres] away is to me a clear and finished piece of work, though the sights of my rifle would now have to be adjusted with the aid of field glasses.

But I was made to stop swaggering about my long-distance sight when Trumper put his bat to the ball. I used to find myself guessing and I nearly always guessed wrong. I predicted a square cut as the ball flashed through the air, and then the ball would go in the air in front of cover-point. I was worse fogged by the strokes to the 'on' and hopelessly baffled by the square leg hits . . . As I watched, I got desperately anxious to analyse the inner workings of the batsman's mind, or the thing it was that was causing the man's mood.

*Guessing; fogged; hopelessly baffled*: in Trumper's hands, batting has become a mystery, inscrutable even to a purported expert, 'too exact for the ordinary eye to follow'. It is not a passage that Grace could have inspired, or really any contemporary bar Ranjitsinhji – admiration tinged with wonder and psychological speculation. It is a step beyond even the insistences of Noble and Davis, that to see Trumper was sufficient to grasp his greatness. The more Trevor sees, the less he feels he understands. Unable to make sense of the method, he falls back on contemplation of the man, in whom there must be something, in his 'mind' or in his 'mood', to make him play in such a way.

•

Was there? Funnily enough, for once in the annals of this enigmatic cricketer, there *is* an accompanying, corroborative record – personal, contemporaneous, utterly authentic, and read in its life span by only a handful of people. Trumper's diary of the 1902 tour, a tiny volume bound in limp black morocco, is now kept in conditions of exacting hygiene at the Melbourne Cricket Club Museum. To read it, one must visit a cold underground room at the MCG where a gloved museum staff member turns the pages.

Handed down the generations of the Trumper family, it was first publicised by Ashley Mallett, who drew on it for his *Trumper* (1985), describing it as a cricket find equivalent to 'stumbling on the Lost City of Atlantis'. In fact, the diarist was almost comically succinct about his experiences. After the first day's training in the Nursery at Lord's, for example, the Australians attended the biblical epic *Ben-Hur*, a Drury Lane replica of the Broadway production that ran twenty-one years. The famous chariot race involved 30 tonnes of horseflesh and vehicles: the horses galloped on treadmills and the chariot wheels were turned by electric rubber rollers while a cyclorama revolved in the opposite direction and fans swirled clouds of dust. The production was also noted for its 'bright-haired and buxom damsels' wearing 'leopard-skin bodices' including gorgeous, pouting Nora Kerin as Esther. Trumper: 'Thursday 1 May: Practice all day. Went to Ben-Hur at night – Drury Lane.'

For the coronation, the cricketers had a premium vantage: out of several invitations, Wardill accepted one from eighty-eight-year-old Baroness Burdett-Coutts, whom the new monarch regarded as 'the most remarkable woman in the kingdom' after a lifetime applying her private banking fortune to charitable works in the East End. She and the Australians now leaned out the same windows in Piccadilly from which the baroness had watched Victoria's coronation in 1838; afterwards she presented each player with a Coronation Medal, which caused excitement in Australia. 'Why should not the

Baroness Burdett-Coutts adopt Vic Trumper?' asked a columnist in *The Arrow*. Trumper: 'Saturday 9 August: Coronation. Baroness Burdett-Coutts. Good view of show. Disappointed. Had lunch there. Saw decorations. Not nearly as good as ours' (presumably a patriotic reference to the 8-kilometre parade to the Federation Pavilion in Centennial Park for the proclamation of the Commonwealth of Australia on 1 January 1901).

Yet there *is* a glint of a man here – and, perhaps surprisingly, it is of a certain steel. Trumper enumerates his likes and dislikes briefly but frankly. Rain, mentioned on half the first fifty days, is a curse ('Nothing but rain'; 'More rain. Miserable'; 'Spent rather miserable day'; 'Rained all day . . . played cards'). Theatre and music hall were tersely reviewed ('Good show'; 'Not bad'; 'Passable'; 'Horrible'; 'Rotten'). There is excitement, especially after Test victories at Bramall Lane ('Hurras. Won match. Glorious. All drunk. Left for Birmingham. Arrived 12 p.m.') and Old Trafford ('Glorious time', then the next day 'all have sore heads'). There is also boredom and weariness ('Very tired'; 'All dog tired'; 'Too tired to go out'; 'Dodged about and done nothing'; 'Glad Tests all over').

Of his own performances, Trumper is typically economical. What did he make of his triumph at Old Trafford? 'Thursday 24 July: Wet wicket. Fourth Test. Won toss, made 299. Self 104. RAD 50. 1st W 135. England 5 for 70. Tate 1st Test. Fire G Peak and Coy.'* But he cares all right. That terse 'Self 104' recalls Donald Bradman's matter-of-fact diary entry after the first day of the Headingley Test twenty-eight years later, when he emulated Trumper in scor-

---

* 'RAD' was Reg Duff, whose opening partnership with Trumper was worth 135 in seventy-eight minutes; 'Tate' was Fred Tate, playing his only Test, at the end of which he would be bowled to give Australia a three-run victory; 'G Peak' was the name of a warehouse next to the Australians' Grand Hotel lodgings that went up in smoke overnight, rather interrupting their preparations.

ing a hundred before lunch, then expanded it into a triple hundred: 'Archie [Jackson] out for 1. I followed and at stumps was 309 not out, breaking the previous highest score in Anglo-Australian Tests. Reached my 2000 runs for the season. To hotel in evening for dinner and wrote letters, thence to bed.' Nor does the comparison with Bradman end there: Trumper emerges as similarly achievement-driven. For much of the 1902 season, he and the Englishman Abel were neck and neck in the aggregates: Abel was first to 1000, Trumper first to 2000. Trumper was aware of Abel's progress, annoyed that he 'missed [the] bus' when he got out for 92 in a high-scoring game against Gloucestershire, vexed to follow 105 with 86 against MCC because he 'wanted double century', and not entirely displeased when Monty Noble against Sussex fell 17 runs short of surpassing the score he had made at the same venue three years earlier ('MAN out for 284 . . . Still have record'). That absorption of Trumper into an anglicised amateur tradition, then, was very much in beholders' eyes; at least at this stage, he was a young man of ambition, striving to make his name.

In general, of course, the diary is valued for what it is rather than what it contains – such is the nature of the trade in historic relics. When it was auctioned at Christie's in Melbourne in August 1997, the diary attracted several aggressive bidders, including Steve Waugh, then on tour in England. The successful purchaser was also from the far side of the world, the prodigious English collector John McKenzie outlaying nearly $30 000. But before McKenzie could secure his investment, the Australian Ministry for the Arts placed the diary on the Movable Cultural Heritage Prohibited Exports Register, which exists for 'objects of exceptional cultural importance, whose export would significantly diminish Australia's cultural heritage' – on par with the shoulder guard from Ned Kelly's armour, the

'King of the West' gold nugget, and a cat-o'-nine-tails once wielded by the master of the brig *Supply*. Which is curiously fitting: because among many things on which the diary provides no information is how close Trumper came in 1902 to being culturally exported himself.

•

Australia's tour was in the black by early July 1902 – that is, the team had repaid its £900 advance from the Melbourne CC, and was busily building the bank balance it would distribute among its members. With news of the cessation of hostilities in the Boer War, the team also felt able to entertain an invitation to play three Tests in South Africa on the way home, at a guaranteed profit of £2000. Other possibilities were also opening. After the game against Sussex finished at Hove on 2 August, Trumper lingered on his own for a spell at Markwell's Royal Hotel in Brighton amid a sibilance of whispers that he was being courted by various English counties, notably Lancashire and Surrey – which would entail him serving a period of residential qualification before playing, and essentially require him to give Test cricket up. The weekly magazine *Cricket* aggregated the rumours comprehensively, and whimsically:

a. That Trumper has had two offers, each worth £350 a year, on condition that he will qualify for a certain county;

b. that he intends to return to Australia, where his income is £150 a year derived from an office under Government;

c. that he will play in 1904 for Surrey;

d. that he will qualify for Lancashire, for which he will play in 1904;

e. that he will qualify as a professional; that he will certainly remain an amateur; and that no offers whatever have been made to him.

Not that you would sense any of the foregoing from the cheerfully mundane tone of Trumper's diary around this time:

Sunday 3 August: Went down to pier and heard band on promenade. Windy and cold.

Monday 4 August: Monday, pier. Heard band, Devil's Dyke in afternoon [an earthwork on the South Downs, a noted beauty spot]. On pier at night.

Tuesday 5 August: Swim. Heard band. Bus ride to Chalk Cliffs of Old England. Band 11.30, 3.30, 7.45.

Wednesday 6 August: Left for Southampton. Arrived 5.10. Saw King's train leaving Portsmouth. Good hotel. New and smells of paint. Team arrived 9 p.m. Letters at G sent for.

Only the very last line hints at other than innocent amusements. Yet the very next morning, a number of articles appeared bruiting Trumper's recruitment by a county club – the favourite seemed to be Surrey, with the bait of an assistant secretaryship. By the press the idea was received unenthusiastically, albeit not because Trumper might be lost to Australia, but because he might play in England *as an amateur* – worse, one of those amateurs paid by their county as an official. The arguments were various. London's *Daily Telegraph* exclaimed that such positions should be the prerogative of *Englishmen*: 'It is one thing for a county to find a position for one of its own men who, without some assistance, could not afford to give up the summer months to first-class cricket, but quite another to bid high for the services of a cricketer quite unconnected with the county because he happens at the moment to be the best bat in the world.' Sheffield's *Daily Telegraph* complained that such positions were *professional* in all but name: 'Surely the MCC will step in and with so clear a case before it will declare that any man who takes over what is virtually an honorary post as the reward of his qualifying must play as a professional or not at all. Shoddy amateurism has begun to stink in this country very much, and there is no wish to increase it in any way. Trumper would do well for the sake of his popularity were he to promptly give the lie to the present rumour.' The gossipy Home Gordon in *The Sportsman*, who reported 'good reason for thinking that the great Australian cricketer will in 1904 appear for Surrey', thought that Trumper would be welcome, but only as a professional – not, ahem, that there was anything wrong in that:

> I am expressing the opinion of more than one prominent
> amateur when I say it is believed he is too good a sportsman to
> be ashamed of owning he is earning a living as a cricketer, and
> to that honourable calling he will give new lustre. To add here
> any panegyric on his ability would be superfluous, but it may be
> mentioned that he is personally a real good fellow, full of generous
> enthusiasm, keenness and a healthy manliness which wins for him
> lots of friends.

Trumper made a scratchy 18 that morning and diarised that he felt 'horribly out of form'. His failure was regarded by others as signifying an uneasy mind. In addition to approaches from counties, he was said to be under offer from Joe Darling for South Australia and Ben Wardill for Victoria. Reports grew openly contradictory. The *Manchester Courier* reported Trumper himself as confirming the probability 'that he would accept one of the offers made to him', there being 'no reason why he should not better his position'. The *Nottingham Evening Post* heard the opposite, adapting Gilbert and Sullivan: 'In spite of all temptations/To belong to other nations/ He remains an – Australian (at least so one hears).' Cartoonist 'Rip' caricatured Trumper scorning moneybags dangling from extended hands.

Gold rush: Trumper declines.

In fact, Trumper was still appraising his options, and quite coolly. This we know from a letter in his fluent, round hand in the archives of the Worcestershire County Cricket Club. Dated the first evening of the Fifth Test at The Oval, it was composed in reply to inquiries about his services by that county's hard-working secretary, Paul Foley. Worcestershire was a recent but ambitious addition to the County Championship. Foley, the scion of ironmasters from Stourbridge, had hauled the club up from among the minor counties by ceaseless endeavours, transforming three sheep pastures in the shadow of Worcester Cathedral into one of England's most picturesque grounds: Trumper had diarised of Worcester as a 'pleasant little city' and of a 'beautiful drive' to nearby Malvern. Foley aimed high: three years earlier he had courted Monty Noble, on the basis of a rumour of the Australian settling in England. Trumper was now disarmingly receptive.

> My Dear Mr Foley,
>
> I am much obliged to you for your courteous letter. I have not decided yet whether I shall stay here or not. Certainly not as a professional with all respects to Home Gordon, who has written us down on all occasions. Should I remain I would just as soon play for your county as any as not only do I like the team both amateur and pro's[sic] but also the town & surrounding district. You have the nucleus of a very good side.

Trumper was dismissive of the reports in circulation: 'The papers are having a lot to say about myself & the strange part of it is that not one of the writers came to me for any information whatsoever & the general public know all about the different articles just as soon as I do.' He was further approving of a sweetener that Foley appears to have offered, probably an assistant secretaryship: 'I am pleased that if I should accept the position I will have something to do in the winter for on no account should I be contented loafing about.' There was, Trumper warned, a potential delay to the beginning of any qualifying residence: 'Our Articles of Agreement state that all the team must go where the majority decide so that should we go to S.Africa or play in Australia on our return I would have to go with them. Our articles are very stiff[;] for instance if we turn up late at a match we are fined £5 for the first offence & stand a chance of being sent home for the second.' Nonetheless, Trumper solicited specifics: 'Could you make me a definite offer with a guarantee for a certain number of years & also let me know what qualifications it would be necessary for me to put in.'

It is a friendly, frank, intelligent letter, socially aware in its dismissal of professionalism, culturally comfortable with the idea of his services being pursued. The little asperity about garrulous Gordon and the knowing jest about the press strike a note of confidentiality, but the words are confident, assured – the same spirit, one presumes, that Trumper took into his next such encounter, with Allen Taylor.*

Taylor was a self-made hardwood timber magnate who had just ended five years as lord mayor of Annandale and would twice serve as lord mayor of Sydney – part of his legacy, perpetuated in the square bearing his name, would be clearing Trumper's Darlinghurst of its worst slums. A visitor to England that summer, Taylor was evidently disquieted by what he was reading. On 14 August, Sydney's *Evening News* reported that Taylor had cabled his business partner good news: 'Glad to say, private offer to Trumper to come back and remain in Sydney, has been accepted to-day.' However, 'no details' could be given, and they never were. On returning to Australia, both parties briefly acknowledged an agreement. Taylor divulged that 'in about another hour' his offer 'might have been too late'; Trumper stated that rather than sign a contract he had accepted his benefactor's 'word as a gentleman'; *Wisden*'s editor, Sydney Pardon, expressed satisfaction that the initiative had fallen through, as it 'would have

---

* It was not the end of Trumper's involvement with Worcestershire, for he recommended to the county Toowoomba-born Jack Cuffe, a left-arm medium-pacer who had played once for NSW. After a two-year residency, Cuffe, playing as a professional, served worthily as the county's first overseas player, taking 738 wickets and making 7476 runs over a decade. After the war, as for many an ex-pro, the pickings were slimmer. Shortly after taking a position as coach of Repton School, C. B. Fry's alma mater, Cuffe drowned himself in the River Trent, aged fifty.

been a paltry and unworthy thing to deprive Australia, by means of a money bribe, of her finest batsman'. It was when Trumper returned to Australia that he opened his first sporting-goods store – with, it's possible, financial support from Taylor. But the biographical trails hereabouts are cold and dead: the diary peters out altogether at this very point, with more than a month of the tour to go.

Why did Trumper shrink from playing county cricket? Was it a reluctance to leave Australia? Was it an aversion to playing openly as a professional, when Australians had scrabbled so hard for social parity? The peace in England was clearly uneasy. While Trumper's batting had delighted and enchanted, there remained clear reservations about his levitating above his station. The pragmatism of Trumper's correspondence with Foley suggests that when it came to it, the simplest explanation is best: he accepted what was, for all sorts of reasons, a better offer, from which he and his chroniclers then turned away, almost by mutual agreement, gentlemen not discussing other gentlemen's financial affairs. And into the spaces left by unsaid words were deposited the sentiments, assertions and conclusions of others.

•

Much of what has been handed down about Trumper at this peak of his career is actually not contemporaneous at all: it was set down in the tranquillity of later memoirs and musings, partly by participants, but most importantly by one eyewitness, who made it a motif in his emergence as cricket's most acclaimed writer.

Neville Cardus's writing about Trumper was of a special intensity: the Australian was, he said, 'first of my heroes – first in point of time, first in affections for all time'. He saw Trumper, he admitted, 'only three or four times', but never tired of describing him, and in a very particular way, for not a word did he compose while his hero was alive. In the summer of 1902, Cardus was fourteen, just growing aware of the music, art and literature that would shape his critical sensibilities and baroque prose; not for another seventeen years would he become 'Cricketer' of the *Manchester Guardian*, by which time Trumper was dead. Cardus was fated, then, always to write about Trumper in the nostalgic tense – and in so doing, to look back on his unformed self:

> As I look back on my boyhood and try to think of all the formative influences that made me a man of some awareness to the things of the imagination, I realise the power of three strangely diverse forces, each evocative of colour and romance – the music of Wagner, Turner's canvas 'The Fighting Temeraire', and Victor Trumper. I do not hesitate, at this high prime of my life, to write the name of Victor Trumper along with those two immortals of a higher plane of artistic activity. Victor was as much an artist in cricket, as much an inspiration to an impressionable urchin of Manchester, as any Turner or Wagner. It doesn't matter, really, in what direction or calling the spirit of genius takes its flights; I would no more forget Trumper's batsmanship than I would forget gorgeous sunsets, cloud-capped mountains, sonorous cadences of verse and symphony, or the full bloom of the rose.

Cardus's origins are as obscure as those of his Australian hero: he barely knew his mother, a prostitute; he never knew his father, her client; he was raised first by grandparents, then by a colourful aunt, in a slum quarter of Manchester. How Cardus came to see Trumper at the Old Trafford Test on 24 July he explained over and over with variations, starting with *The Summer Game* (1929). In *Good Days* (1934), he 'played truant from school to see it'. In *Australian Summer* (1937), he colourfully described obtaining his sixpence for the turnstile by selling 'a volume of Coleridge's poems' from his grandfather's library: 'I remember that when I went to sell the volume, feeling a criminal, I noticed one of the poems was called "Remorse"; to this day I cannot understand how the poems got into my grandfather's library, which began with the Bible and ended with the *Sporting Chronicle Handicap Book*.' In *Autobiography* (1947), he still more colourfully recalled his cricket watching being enabled by his aunt winning a breach-of-promise suit against Manchester's Turkish consul.

Given his admitted tendency to write what was 'true to character' rather than true to fact, whether Cardus was at Old Trafford *at all* may be open to some doubt. But that day at Old Trafford was particularly appealing to Cardus for pitting two of his great favourites against one another. England's captain was the superbly haughty Archie MacLaren, one of those permanently impecunious English amateurs with champagne tastes on a beer budget. Balzac, Carlyle, Wagner, Sir Henry Irving, Sir Thomas Beecham: Cardus would invoke them all in his various descriptions of MacLaren, who 'lighted a fire in me never to go out'. A favourite story, repeated at intervals with the usual variations, involved a dinner, circa the 1920s, at which Cardus and other guests chaffed MacLaren about being too defensive on the first morning at Old Trafford those many years before:

> We challenged MacLaren: 'Why Archie, you must have slipped
> a bit when you allowed Trumper to win the 1902 rubber on a turf
> nearly waterlogged in the outfield. Did you place too many men
> deep, and allow Victor to pick up the runs through the gaps near
> the wicket?'

MacLaren, who adored an argument, rose to the bait; he took lumps of sugar out of the basin and set them all over the table, saying 'Gaps be damned! Good God, I knew my man – Victor had half a dozen strokes for the same kind of ball. I exploited the inner ring and outer ring – a man here, a man there, and another man covering him.' (He banged the lumps of sugar down one by one, punctuating his luminous discourse.) 'I told my bowlers to pitch on the short side to the off; I set my heart and brain on every detail of our policy. Well, in the third over of the morning, Victor hit two balls straight into the practice ground, high over the screen, behind the bowler. I couldn't very well have had a man fielding in the practice ground, now could I?'

To Cardus, Trumper was a 'comet that flashed into my ken': 'Trumper, when I was young, made me fall in love with Australia. When I was 14 or 15, my chances of getting to Australia seemed as remote as my chance of becoming Lord Chancellor.' When this changed, and Cardus became England's most feted cricket writer, that first sight took on the quality of an omen, and of Trumper he remained ever protective. By the time Cardus commenced writing his own life story, the attachment was the keener for him actually being in Trumper's old neighbourhood: the slum boy, the prostitute's son, was sojourning in Kings Cross as music critic for the *Sydney Morning Herald* and host of the ABC's Sunday night 'The Enjoyment of Music', his bolthole from the privations of World War II. Visiting places that were part of the Trumper story was for Cardus like touring his own imagination: 'I never trod the grass of Paddington Oval without a warming of the heart.' By then, as we shall see, Cardus had elevated the cricket of his youth to a glorious and unsullied idyll, with Trumper its supreme stylist.

Perhaps it was also the identification of one young man who had transcended his unpromising circumstances by virtue of a special flair with another. 'He could not, had he tried, have played a plebeian stroke,' thought Cardus of Trumper – just as Cardus had hoisted himself by the bootstraps of his prose. 'I once called Neville the "Victor Trumper of cricket writing",' recalled his friend Jack Fingleton. 'He thanked me for the compliment.'

•

Victor Trumper and 1902: so inseparable, so ungraspable, so historic, so mythic. And with a last set of relics we have yet to grapple. Two years after events, two photographs of Trumper in action *were* published, small and indistinct, in *C. B. Fry's Magazine*. You would not know they were of Trumper were it not for their captions, so minuscule does his figure appear from the camera's vantage on the pavilion balcony at The Oval on 11 August, the first day of the Fifth Test. In one, Trumper looks to be going back and across; in the other, he seems to have hit over the top of the ball. Like Trumper's diary, they are of interest primarily because of their association with him; unlike Trumper's diary, they portended a revolution.

# 4

# 'THE CHAMPION THEORIST'

'I don't think you can really say you have seen something
until you have taken a photograph of it, which reveals all the details
you would not otherwise have noticed – and which in most
cases cannot even be seen.'
– EMILE ZOLA (1901)

In E. W. Hornung's short story 'Gentlemen and Players' (1899), the cricketing amateur cracksman A. J. Raffles and his offsider Bunny Manders are guests at a Dorset country house. The weekend centres on games of cricket organised by their host Lord Amersteth; Raffles and Bunny have eyes only for the priceless sapphire adorning Lady Melrose. Nervous and edgy, Bunny finds himself after dinner in wearisome company:

Lastly in the billiard room they had a great and lengthy pool table, while I sat aloof and chafed more than ever in the company of a very serious Scotchman, who had arrived since dinner, and who would talk of nothing but the recent improvements in instantaneous photography. He had not come to play in the matches (he told me), but to obtain for Lord Amersteth such a series of cricket photographs as had never been taken before; whether as an amateur or a professional photographer I was unable to determine. I remember, however, seeking distraction in little bursts of resolute attention to the conversation of this bore. And so at last the long ordeal ended; glasses were emptied, men said goodnight and I followed Raffles to his room.

The locquacious photographer proves to be a detective in disguise. Inspector Mackenzie of the Yard is on the trail of *another* thief with designs on the sapphire. The character's real-life inspiration is unknown: Hornung was himself much taken with photography, later blending it into a murder mystery, *The Camera Fiend* (1911). But it's tempting to imagine his having had an early encounter with George Beldam.

Descended from Huguenots who had crossed the Channel from Picardy in the seventeenth century, Beldam was born 1 May 1868. His father, Asplan, was a maritime designer in a Thames shipyard, and shortly established his own engineering company to address a very particular problem. Most boilers were then poorly insulated, and unable to operate at more than 30–40 pounds per square inch. In May 1876, Asplan patented a form of 'packing', combining canvas, felt and folded metal interleaved with grease, that increased boiler pressure three and four times. He advertised his Beldam Packing & Rubber Company with the SS *Stirling Castle*, which won the Great Tea Races of 1882 and 1883, steaming from

'He must know how it is done': George Beldam.

China while bulging with tea in record times. By then, Asplan and wife Elizabeth were raising two sons and two daughters in a large house and grounds near Brentford, Acton Lodge. George, the oldest, went to study engineering at Cambridge, where he attended St Peter's and captained Peterhouse at cricket, football and tennis before joining the family firm.

By class and inclination, then, Beldam was an amateur. He played amateur cricket for Luton CC, amateur football for Brentford FC, amateur golf at Walton Heath and Royal Mid-Surrey golf clubs. He would remain all his life a serial enthusiast for pastimes, from fly fishing to watercolour art, his canvases exhibiting a partiality to moody landscapes and majestic windjammers – ironically of the kind his company was helping to render obsolete. Then there was photography.

Photography was then making a comeback as an amateur pursuit, thanks to the invention of the easy-to-use dry gelatine plate and pre-mixed developing chemicals. The new amateur photographers were unlike the pioneers of old; their bible, *Amateur Photographer*, aimed at hobbyists, dispensing technical advice at a beginner's level. But the magazine also became a home for debates around amateurism itself, rather like those in cricket. 'The distinction between an Amateur and Professional is, the latter lives by his art, and the former does not,' pronounced the editor, with a Marylebone-like qualification. 'The payment of expenses is a side question.' Photography should be approached, another correspondent thought, with a sporting spirit: 'Well to us amateurs, photography is but a relaxation – a scientific Sport, but a Sport all the same.' He might well have been speaking for Beldam.

These new amateurs tugged photography in unforeseen directions. In December 1890, one enthusiast, civil servant George Davison, exhibited his famous 'The Onion Field': a misty, pastoral vision captured through a pinhole in a piece of sheet metal rather than with a conventional lens, then printed on rough paper so that it resembled an impressionist painting. Its effect was galvanising: Davison would lead a secession from the Photographic Society called the Linked Ring Brotherhood, the vanguard of a movement known respectfully as pictorialism and less respectfully as 'the fuzzy wuzzies' for the way practitioners used substances like gum bichromate and carbon pigment to soften reality's hard edges.

Beldam corresponds to no movement, and never seems to have fraternised with other photographers – his overlapping social circles would be athletes, artists and businessmen. When he first took up a camera in his mid-twenties, his subjects were friends and family, and his earliest cricket photograph a joke on his uncle, infamous in games on the family lawn for never accepting an lbw dismissal:

One day I took a snapshot of him, with my father standing behind the wicket in an attitude of appealing to the umpire. I told my father how to stand, and then turning to my uncle I said, 'There is no need for me to tell you what to do. Just imagine that you have been given out leg-before-wicket.' The result was a snapshot in which the ball is just hitting his leg (placed well in front of the wicket) while he looks up with an air of greatest surprise and indignation.

It is a charming photograph, and a foreshadowing one. For although a jest, it concerns those instants in cricket that otherwise impress only on the mind's eye; and while it is contrived, it seeks after a spontaneity, a naturalness ('There is no need for me to tell you what to do'). The wicketkeeper and batsman are oppositely engaged; the ball, having struck the pad, floats incriminatingly; the photographer is, as it were, the umpire. And if he was as yet unaware, Beldam the photographer had his subject. That subject was movement.

'A snapshot': Beldam's first cricket image.

•

In photography's foundational days, movement had cheated the camera because of the prolonged exposures necessary to obtain a satisfactory image. Movement had, of course, always cheated art, too, but traditional forms of painting, drawing, printmaking and sculpture had evolved an intricate visual language to convey motion, like the aforementioned concentration on 'memorably perceived' phases. Photography was condemned to repeat reality, in all its unpredictability.

A small vernacular movement, 'instantaneous photography', took this as a challenge, yielding erratic but evocative results. In October 1862, for example, an adventurous commercial photographer, Valentine Blanchard, exhibited an image of London's New Oxford Street, captured by means of a wide-aperture stereo camera mounted on a 'mobile studio' – a carriage with a viewing platform and a darkroom. 'Omnibuses, carts, cabs, wagons, and foot-passengers in shoals in active movement, are all "arrested",' reported the *British Journal of Photography*:

> In the immediate foreground is a man, without his coat, wheeling a
> barrow, his left leg poised in mid-air, in the act of stepping . . . One
> individual in a black suit, with his hands in his pockets, and looking
> on excellent terms with himself, is sauntering towards the spectator.
> The whole scene is full of life, and the photography leaves nothing
> to be desired.

The instantaneous also touched Victorians sentimentally. Two hundred and fifty thousand copies were sold of a bizarre curio of a crying baby that first appeared as a plate in Charles Darwin's *The Expression of the Emotions in Man and Animals* (1872): Oscar Rejlander's small, indistinct, redrawn and rephotographed image came to be known as

'Ginx's Baby', from the title of a popular satire on urban poverty and its relief by Edward Jenkins.

Even then the photographer who would do most to unlock the instant was starting out in the United States. In 1872, émigré Englishman Eadweard Muybridge was hired by Californian railroad magnate Leland Stanford to ascertain whether all four hooves of a moving horse were ever simultaneously airborne. Equine painters had traditionally presented their subjects *ventre à terre* (belly to the ground), legs fore-and-aft like a rocking horse. Within a year, Muybridge had captured, on a wet plate at one-500th of a second, a silhouette of Stanford's champion racehorse, Occident, in 'unsupported transit'; he carried on his experiments at Sacramento Bay Track and Stanford's Palo Alto estate until he had proof in photo sequences from a battery of twelve cameras. 'The machine cannot lie,' Stanford felt able to pronounce.

The findings caused a sensation, not least among equine painters, who either fell repentantly in line or looked studiously the other way on the grounds that a mechanical view was inimical to a human artwork; they also caused a *froideur* between photographer and patron over credit for the discovery. Muybridge relocated to the University

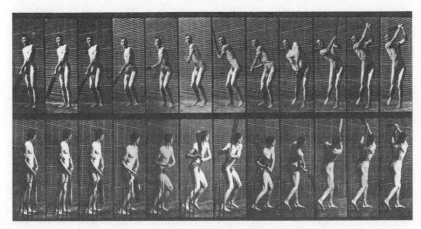

Shotmaker: cricket gets the Muybridge treatment.

93

of Pennsylvania, where he used another battery of cameras for a sweeping survey of human and animal motion generating tens of thousands of 'seriates': bison cantering; big cats prowling; boys leap-frogging; ballet dancers pirouetting; baseballers slugging; discus throwers propelling; chickens 'startled by a torpedo'; a 340 lb (154 kg) nude woman rising to her feet. Muybridge used nudes extensively, including one identified as 'the best all-round cricketer in the University of Pennsylvania', purveying overarm and round-arm bowling, playing the back cut and the straight drive – the last uncannily anticipated one of Beldam's later Trumper images. Whether Beldam was actually aware of Muybridge's 'seriates' is obscure, but moot. He was certainly, as we shall see, exercised by questions of actuality and beauty – the point of intersection between photography's documentary and artistic impulses. And his work would run entirely against the grain.

•

By the 1890s, photography had made inroads into a number of sports, but in the main those where action was predictable and proximate, such as the finishes of horse and cycle races, athletics meetings and rowing events. In cricket, photography flourished in only one corner: portraiture. The Brighton firm of E. Hawkins & Co., for example, had established itself in the old premises of Mason's 'Repository of Art', and gained the patronage of Lord Sheffield, who regularly hosted cricket teams, including Australians, on his nearby estate. It became the custom for cricketers visiting Hove to pose for Hawkins & Co.'s Thomas Foster, usually standing by a set of stumps, sometimes in a batting stance, sometimes holding a ball high in an extended hand. Reproduced as cabinet cards, the bigger, thicker successor to *cartes de visite*, these photographs became the chief way by which cricketers were popularly known. Hawkins never had a greater seller than Foster's 1893 photograph of Grace stooping weightily over his bat, which the old-timer Richard Daft acclaimed as cricket's definitive image: 'When Dr Grace is no more, future generations must be shown these portraits, for it will be the next best thing to having seen the player himself.' All the same, Daft was conscious of such pictures stopping short of true action. He looked forward to the day when 'good, large instantaneous photographs may be taken of players in the field, and actually taking part in a match', which would 'do more to describe the play of the men themselves than pages of writing would do'.

Until then, cricket would have to wait, somewhat frustratedly. In 1895, the artist Harry Furniss went to Lord's for the Gentlemen v Players match and saw forty-six-year-old Grace peel off the seventh

Still life: Hawkins' Grace.

of the nine hundreds of his 'Indian summer'. Furniss returned to his studio 'with the massive form of "WG" well imprinted upon my brain', and dashed off 'a hundred sketches from memory' that would compose *A Century of Grace* (1896) – probably the liveliest and most charming of all such illustrations. Furniss confessed disappointment nonetheless. It was, he concluded, 'impossible to make a satisfactory picture of our national game' from 'a crowd of ordinary sightseers in the foreground and also in the distance, and between these a large expanse of green grass, with a few white spots'. Worse, nor was photography up to the mark:

> Of course, the ordinary photograph of the cricketer, whether he sits or stands at ease, is a portrait. But what about him in action? If he is told to pose before a camera – if he is a batsman, he fails to get the proper swing, as he is only watching the lens, and not inspired to the correct action by seeing the ball flying towards him from the muscular arm of a Lohmann or a Richardson . . . No, the photograph must be taken unawares, and perhaps before this little preface is published we may find depicted by the Cinematograph some of our well-known cricketers at play. But these have to be taken at a distance, when the game is in progress, and then enlarged; and I would like to see anyone venture on to a cricket field during the progress of some good match! The poor photographer would have to provide himself with dummy camera, as used when photographing at the Zoo.

But others were now being exercised by these challenges – including the two most glamorous names in the game.

•

Sketch life: Furniss's Grace.

The cricket celebrityhood conferred on Ranjitsinhji and C. B. Fry by their feats and by *The Jubilee Book of Cricket* (1897) brought complications. In 1897, Ranji fathered an illegitimate child with the daughter of his former Cambridge tutor; in 1898, Fry married another man's long-term mistress. The latter was a most remarkable woman. In her teens, Beatrice Sumner had been a famous beauty, a brilliant huntress, and an object of the ardour of wealthy banker Charles Hoare, fifteen years her senior and already a father of five. Increasingly desperate efforts were made by their families to prevent a relationship, but on her twenty-first birthday, Beatie broke from her guardians, reunited with Hoare, and bore him a son, then a daughter. During the scandalous court case that followed, the judge described Beatie as having 'suffered a fall from which no woman could live to recover'. Yet by sheer willpower she clambered back into respectable circles, thanks to an old barque that Hoare turned into a boys' naval college at Hamble – and also to Fry.

On TS *Mercury*, the overpowering influence was Beatie, a wintry martinet whose religiosity was exacerbated by a passion for Wagner: Hoare built her a 300-seat theatre modelled on Bayreuth featuring a giant crucifix with a life-size Christ whom visitors were required to salute. In the fashion of Hornung's Lord Amersteth, Hoare also enjoyed hosting famous cricketers, and thirty-five-year-old Beatie diarised fatefully after one visit: 'Charles Fry came to play cricket today. I like Fry.' Fry's marriage to the woman he referred to as 'my madame' was immediately complicated by her bearing a third child who was probably Hoare's, but at least relieved him of the burdens of teaching. His lapidary turns of phrase began appearing in *Windsor Magazine, Lloyd's News, Westminster Gazette, Athletic News*, the *Daily Express*, and the popular boys' magazine *The Captain*. As Fry's first biographer recalled: 'Very often if you broke into his hotel at ten o'clock, when other players were at the play or the cardtable, C. B. Fry, in a loose flannel suit with the sleeves turned up, would be found in his bedroom turning out copy.' From such bedrooms soon emerged something peculiarly his own.

Fry's *The Book of Cricket* (1899), a collection of pen portraits of his contemporaries, was less comprehensive than the *Jubilee Book* but rather breezier, even humorous when the author limned himself in the third person:

> In his earlier days Mr Fry was a stiff, ungainly bat . . . Mr Fry
> is aware that from the moment he had the privilege of playing with
> Kumar Shri Ranjitsinhji he began to improve his game – a fact
> which, when the absolute diversity of their styles is remembered,
> emphasises the value of observing the methods of a great
> player . . . He is no cutter, and a very intermittent off-driver.

He plays chiefly with his shoulders and fore-arms; not enough wrist. He has confidence in his back play which is not altogether justified. He would do better with more patience, and with a little more judgement in hitting. He prefers not to refer to such bowling as he once did. He is generally fond of fielding, and is ready to go anywhere. He is thought by his friends to be slightly too theoretical.

The middle of the same page contained a vivid image: as Fry leaned into an on-drive, a ball hurtled towards the camera. The *Jubilee Book* had relied on demonstration poses by leading cricketers of the day, profuse but static and barely distinguishable from postcard portraits; *The Book of Cricket* was about action. A blurred ball energised Billy Murdoch's lusty square cut, Pelham Warner's firm punch, Archie MacLaren's on-side prod, the defensive shots of Bobby Abel and Arthur Shrewsbury; speed smudged the arms of Hugh Trumble and Monty Noble; Jim Kelly caught an unseen batsman at the wicket; Harry Wood stumped a genuflecting Fry.

Photographer William Rouch normally specialised in blood-stock; the impetus was assuredly Fry's. Back in April 1892 when Fry had broken the British long-jump record at Queen's Club, his leap had been captured by a member of Stearn Brothers, a family-run photographic firm from Cambridge. Fry loved the image, in which he appeared almost to be hovering as a top-hatted official looked on – it would take pride of place in his autobiography. In *The Book of Cricket*, he was seeking a similar vigour, enhancing the narrative vitality of the images with zesty captions. Albert Trott walked back with a knowing look ('Now for that fast one'), rolled his arm over vigorously ('Whizz!') and cupped a return catch ('That's what I bowl for'). Lancashire's captain George Bardswell was shown cogitating about whether to use his fastest bowler, Arthur Mold ('Shall I put

Man of action: C. B. Fry meets the camera.

to one-1000th of a second. It was this camera that he took to The Oval in August 1902, where he took those two snaps of a far-off Trumper at the crease. Fossickings among Beldam's surviving plates by the cricket-book dealer Michael Down have recently exposed a little more: six never-before-seen Beldam photographs of Trumper in the nets. The print of a seventh photograph evidently in the same sequence is contained in a scrapbook in the possession of the prodigious collector Roger Mann, itself extracted from a scrapbook kept by former Middlesex wicketkeeper Cecil Headlam – such are the feint trails that Beldam left by never cataloguing or annotating his own work. But if Headlam's caption on that seventh photograph can be believed, the practice session in question, at which Beldam also photographed Trumper's colleague Hugh Trumble, was at Lord's preparatory to Australia v Middlesex, a fortnight after The Oval Test.

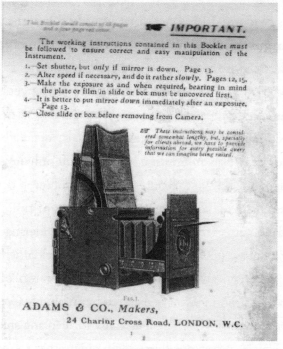

'Important': from the Adams Videx manual.

These are images Beldam never troubled to publish because, again, they're pretty poor. They suggest a photographer still growing accustomed to his apparatus, and to the challenges of composition, exposure and timing. In one photograph, Trumper plays an attractive shot off the hip; in another he is bowled. The photograph of Trumble shows his arm at an intermediate point between release and follow-through. The light is murky. The backdrop is messy. The plates have been damaged by inadequate storage. At this point, then, Beldam was not really a photographer; rather was he an amateur cricketer who owned a camera, a novelty presence, if an engaging one.

In the most appealing of the Lord's sequence, Trumper shapes to play a stroke while looking directly at the camera with a winsome smile, as though engaged by the fun of it all, and perhaps also by Beldam's busy, inquisitive personality. Though not long in the game, Beldam already had a reputation. One of his London County teammates that summer was Leslie Poidevin, a gifted all-round sportsman from Sydney who having represented New South Wales at cricket and tennis had just settled in Manchester to further his medical studies. He also sent off weekly tidbits of interest to J. C. Davis at *The Referee*, and was evidently rather taken by Beldam's slant on the game, his interesting hobby, and his obvious appreciation of Australia's finest cricketer:

> Beldam is one of those thoughtful players – a theorist many people might say, but I prefer to name him a genuine enthusiast – with a fine collection of blades and photographs, and a singularly pleasant, engaging disposition. He is at all times critically observant, everready to pick up something that he may be able to adapt to his own use. He carefully studies the methods of other players, and he is not

content to see and admire Trumper; he must know how it is done, even if he has to ask the brilliant young Paddingtonian himself.

*He must know how it is done*: and this, with Beldam, amounted almost to an obsession.

•

Notwithstanding his experiments at The Oval and at Lord's, Beldam's first real photographic success would be in another sport. In addition to his cricket, he was also a scratch golfer, who introduced a number of cricket teammates to the game, including a quickly enthralled W.G.: 'It ought not to be difficult to hit that little ball lying so still . . . If it were rolled up towards me, I could guarantee to hit it a good distance and in any given direction, but as it lies staring me in the face invitingly, I feel a perfect fool.' Among his friends at Royal Mid-Surrey was the pro, John Henry Taylor, who with Harry Vardon and James Braid formed the game's 'Great Triumvirate'. Beldam struck Taylor in much the same way as he struck Poidevin:

> During my professional life I have come into contact with scores of
> theorists, those eager and almost demented seekers after truth, who
> have endeavoured to prove that if such and such a thing was done,
> something else was bound to happen, a something that would
> reveal the most vital secrets hidden from others who had not the
> courage or desire to probe for them. Mr Beldam was the champion
> theorist. The placing of the fingers on the grip of the club to within
> a fractional part of an inch, the question whether the toes of the
> feet were turned inwards or out was considered of sufficient interest

to set him off on a hunt for information and confirmation; and in the search for what he considered the truth he demonstrated so convincingly that the most hardened sceptic would be forced to acknowledge the rightness of the claim. In addition to this endless quest for rock-bottom divination that became a mania, Mr Beldam was an amateur photographer of genius.

Golf was an excellent photographic subject: distance was no impediment, the ball started from a stationary position, the action was concentrated in a small area. There were already a range of instructional books in which golfers held stiff poses for the purposes of tuition. But what might the camera discern that the human eye could not? With Taylor as adviser and ambassador, Beldam began assembling the bulging portfolio of 'Action-Photographs' of Britain's leading golfers that would compose *Great Golfers: Their Methods at a Glance* (1904).

'Action-Photographs': the very formulation was uncertain, provisional. After all, 'action' implied motion, 'photography' stillness. Beldam abandoned the inverted commas after a while, then gradually dispensed with the hyphen, but remained partial to the capitals, distinguishing the uniqueness of his vision. For in what he was attempting there were no guides, no mentors, not even rivals. The American Charles Conlon, a newspaper proofreader, was just starting out as an amateur photographer of baseball at New York's Polo Grounds, home of the Giants, but his snapshot souvenirs were not nearly so technically ambitious as Beldam's painstaking inquiries into the mysteries of the golf swing.

The trick of it, Beldam established by trial and error, was concentrating on the wrists rather than the club head. In order to compensate for the difference between 'the eye seeing and hand pressing', he also learned to press the Videx's button 'just before I wanted to'. His twenty-four subjects were patient because they were also fascinated. They were not, it turned out, reliable narrators of their own game. Beldam cited the case of Horace Hutchinson, twice Britain's amateur champion, and a celebrated golf critic. Hutchinson swore he had a short swing; 'Action-Photography' proved emphatically otherwise. Often Beldam would ask his subjects to demonstrate a point by striking a pose, only to find that the same point in an actual stroke looked quite different in motion. The conclusion was devastating to prior golf books with their emphasis on static illustration. 'Photographs taken "en pose" are not only worthless from the golfer's point of view, but are very misleading,' concluded Beldam. 'If an amateur champion, and a no less brilliant writer, were led astray, and allowed his years of close observation to be over-ruled – what chance would an ordinary man have?'

*Great Golfers* was an immediate success. 'There will be, I think, a general consensus of opinion as to the extreme excellence of the photographs throughout the book,' opined *Illustrated Sporting and Dramatic News*. 'If this study does not lead to improved form at the links, I for one shall be vastly astonished.' Reviewers were particularly taken with the quasi-scientific air that Beldam introduced to the photographs by posing his subjects on a grid 4 feet × 4 feet (1.2 metres × 1.2 metres) divided by painted lines into sixty-four squares. Beldam's patented linoleum mat, marked in the same fashion so that readers could mimic the greats more exactly, was presently paid the tribute of parody by *Golf Illustrated*'s cartoonist E. W. Mitchell, who transformed it into a griddle in the hands of chef 'Mons Georges Belledame': 'Golfers Grilled at a Glance.'

The most gushing testimonial for *Great Golfers* – 'Not only the book of the month but the best book on golf instruction yet produced' – came in a new publication. *C. B. Fry's Magazine of Action and Outdoor Life*, which commenced publication in April 1904, ran the full gamut of recreations: cricket, football, rugby, tennis, rowing, racing, wrestling, hunting, fishing and motoring. It was the brainchild of the proprietor of *The Captain*. 'Sir George Newnes . . . explained that a monthly magazine is the easiest production imaginable,' recalled Fry. 'I should sit in a comfortable chair with my mind at ease, and select some seven or eight excellent articles sent in for consideration by clever young men such as barristers waiting for briefs.' Beldam became one of those clever young men. To *Fry's* he provided numerous golf and cricket images, previewed the British Open and British Amateur titles, and undertook with Taylor a four-part guide to 'Golf Faults Illustrated', which became the basis of another book.

In addition, Beldam took on a further bold project. He had been approached by Percy Vaile, a flamboyant Auckland lawyer turned 'wanderer on the face of the earth', seeking 'instantaneous photographs' for an instructional book he had dashed off 'in a few days'. And after providing twenty-seven images for Vaile's *Modern Lawn Tennis* (1904), Beldam comprehensively photographed June 1904's All-England Championships for a larger follow-up entitled *Great Lawn Tennis Players: Their Methods Illustrated* (1905).

Despite its 229 images of thirty players, *Great Lawn Tennis Players* proved a less easy temperamental mix than *Great Golfers*. Unlike J. H. Taylor, Vaile was not a champion, even if this diminished the confidence of the views he expressed in London sporting journals, notably *The Field*, not a whit:

> Many players on whose judgement and integrity I would stake
> my – tennis – reputation have assured me that if I had started

much younger, and played a better game, I might even now be a
champion; and I know, without being told, that if I could play it
as well as I know and love it, I might even now be a champion, if
it were not for a trifling want of wind, and no want of that sort of
condition that tennis players are not glad to be without.

The divergence in the collaborators' approaches was reflected in
their prefaces: while Beldam gently cautioned that 'this work is not
to take the place of books on the game written by champions and
experts', Vaile unblushingly declared that 'the true science which
underlies the game of lawn tennis has not yet begun to be realised by
the players of the United Kingdom'. Reviewers, in fact, distinguished
carefully between the contributions of photographer and writer:
even Vaile's own employer, *The Field*, while judging the photographs a 'conspicuous success', dismissed the text as 'very florid',
'very unsound' and in places 'obviously absurd'.

Tennis was in any case merely a passing fancy. Beldam wanted
above all to contribute to cricket. Cricketers, he found, were as
kinaesthetically naive as golfers. One day, he and W.G. were part of a
group playing golf conversing about 'follow-through'. The Champion
scoffed. 'Follow-through'? Who'd ever heard of such a thing? It was
'all bunkum'. 'I could not believe he was in earnest but found that
he was,' Beldam recalled. 'I then told him I would prove by Action
Photographs that he had a follow-through.' They arranged to photograph W.G.'s swings for cricket and golf. The results were conclusive:
'When he [Grace] saw the photographs he had to own that they sur-
prised him, and he must have some kind of follow-through though
he could never have shown anyone what it was.'

What might this imply, Beldam wondered, about prior works of
cricket instruction, even by thinkers as advanced as Fry and Ranji?

The *Jubilee Book* had stressed the efficacy of stationary demonstration: 'The making of nearly all strokes in cricket requires the man to put himself in certain positions if the strokes are to be properly made.' Yet in real life a stroke was not a succession of 'certain positions' into which one 'put' one's self; it was a continuous motion. Surely it had to be illustrated as such. What if you could? What then? The open sesame? The golden way?

Fry was intrigued. *The Book of Cricket* had after all gestured in the same direction. But he was also not quite convinced. His classicist's interests spanned the aesthetic and antiquarian as well as the athletic. For the first issue of *Fry's Magazine* he had visited the octogenarian G. F. Watts, in the last year of the spirited artistic life that had begun with those little cricket sketches for Felix and was now culminating in his colossal equestrian statue 'Physical Energy'. Fry's profile, 'Physical Energy and Mr G. F. Watts, R.A., O.M.', read as a kind of proclamation, extolling art's power to infuse its viewers with 'a fresher-fountained energy', even when they were 'jaded by the cares and earth-ridden by the anxieties of our common day'. The statue, Fry argued, 'typifies the pause, the arrest, the interval between one act of supreme energy and the coming moment of continued action'. He dismissed carpings by some critics that the horse's pose was impossible. Art, argued Fry, was not a literal transcription of nature: 'Physical Energy' was 'a Watts horse and a Watts man, true to the mind and the hand of the maker'.

It was an esoteric diversion for an outdoor sport magazine. Newnes, Fry recalled, detested the piece: 'He smoothed his brown beard and kept repeating through it, "But Mr Fry, why Physical Energy? Why Physical Energy?" Like many other friends of mine who ought to have known better, he could not see any subject properly subscribed to my name except cricket or football.' Fry was

of wristwork, stance and follow-through. It lasted quite a long time, and I do not think we did any more planning that day.

*Wristwork*: this was an insight on which Beldam and Fry agreed – the involvement of the wrists relative to the arms. A powerful stroke had always been identified with a hearty armswing. What Beldam and Fry discerned among the best players were arms relatively compact and close to the body, and hands that remained in roughly the same space; from what they called a 'secondary position', reached at the top of the backlift, it appeared to be the wrists that imparted force and governed placement. The thesis awaited, as it were, the acid test – Fry's own batting ideal.

•

When George Beldam arrived in Brighton to represent Middlesex against Sussex on 25 August 1904, he first kept an appointment – in retrospect an ironic one. Following what had been standard practice among county cricketers for nearly twenty years, he took up his stance and gazed levelly into a Hawkins & Co. camera. To be turned into a cabinet card was a mark of some distinction, a confirmation of the progress he had made in his late cricket flowering. Three days later, Beldam took up the challenge of rendering such images redundant.

Middlesex had the better of the game, Beldam hitting the winning runs. Then he really got to work, returning to the centre of the empty county ground at Hove dressed in his cap, blazer and flannels, spreading his camera gear and erecting his tripod. Ranji put on his pads and assumed his stance; Fry returned from kicking a football with some of the Sussex professionals to bowl a ball; and Beldam started taking photographs, of off-side shots from short mid-wicket,

Frozen: Hawkins's Beldam.

of leg-side shots from short cover. As the report from his bat echoed, Ranji ran through his full repertoire. Boys fetched. Hours passed. Beldam's holder began bulging with 5-inch × 4-inch (13 cm × 10 cm) plates. Fry broke off at one point to take his own photograph of Beldam in action; he also took away, as becomes apparent reading the commentaries he later wrote about each image, a mind's-eye impression of each shot ('It was a good length, medium-pace ball outside the off-stump'; 'The ball rose rather high at the batsman's body' etc.).

Fry would preface these commentaries by quietly reiterating his original objection to 'instantaneous photography'. He had, he wrote, expected to see a 'very remarkable degree of difference' between Ranji and 'what other batsmen do': the still image could not quite do justice to Ranji's capacity for moving 'as if he had no bones'. Otherwise he confessed to being impressed: Beldam showed

'THE CHAMPION THEORIST'

how economically Ranji's arms moved; how coolly Ranji rolled his wrists when cutting; how daintily Ranji crossed his legs in glancing. By one image Fry was exhilarated: his friend 'jumping out to drive', prancing like a warhorse, front foot high off the ground, back toe just grounded, eyes flashing.

Arguably, it was the least natural and most staged of all the strokes – eighty years later, it would be rather deliciously spoofed by the cartoonist Willie Rushton in his book *Marylebone versus the World* (1987). But perhaps it struck Fry as akin to 'Physical Action', capturing the feeling of Ranji at the crease rather than a mere instant, and somehow truer than fact: certainly, as that champion of Valentine Blanchard's had long ago pointed out, there was something uniquely compelling about photography's ability to capture the foot in space, the step in time, the texture of action beyond perception. Whatever the case, alongside a memoir of the day, Fry allocated this 'excellent specimen' of Beldam's 'swift-action photography' a full page in the next edition of *Fry's Magazine*. And he decided, with uncharacteristic restraint, that to the image he had little to add: 'The picture, more or less, speaks for itself.'

•

Beldam's mission at Hove nodded to another dimension of photography – its capacity to preserve for all time. Ranji was shortly to board a ship for India, determined to wrest back his princely inheritance in Nawanagar; his Test career was over; he would not play again for four years, and only one half-hearted season thereafter. Beldam had an eye to posterity, too. Having documented Grace, he also photographed Grace's erstwhile rival Fred Spofforth, now settled in England as manager of the Star Tea Company. Donning his creams at Hampstead CC, the fifty-one-year-old attested the vigour of his retirement regime. 'For my own part, I am still a believer in practice; and scarcely a day passes in the winter that I do not go through the delivery of at least twelve balls,' Spofforth explained. 'By this I mean that without any ball in my hand I bowl at least 72 balls a week with all the power I have, at some imaginary crack batsman.' As Beldam's shutter clicked, Spofforth bowled to eternity with an energetic fluency.

By now, Beldam's survey was all-consuming: the diary of his painter friend Henry Tuke includes a reference to a winter salon at Boston Lodge attended by Fry, Hal Ludlow and Chevallier Tayler at which there was 'great talk on the artistic aspects of cricket figures in action'. Beldam already seems to have had in mind a batting *and* a bowling book, as he commissioned Tuke to paint both W. G. Grace and Spofforth for frontispieces. The batting book would come first, the structure a hybrid of *Great Golfers* and *Great Lawn Tennis Players*: a joint preface about batting bookended by a Beldam epilogue about photography; between them a section dedicated to particular strokes ('Strokes Illustrated'), and a section concentrated on a batting elite ('Individualities'). Among these there would be the past master Grace, the Test stars Fry, Ranji, MacLaren, Jessop and Jackson, the professional stalwarts Hayward and Hirst alongside amateur stylists Lionel Palairet and R. E. Foster; and there would be – there would have to be – Victor Trumper.

# 5

# 'SOME DAY SOMEONE WILL PAINT HIS PORTRAIT'

'In Victor Trumper we have seen the very poetry and heard
the deep and wonderful music of batsmanship. Not the structures of a great
mentality, not the argument of logic, but a sweet and simple strain of beauty,
the gift of the gods alone. Stylish in the highest sense, orthodox,
yet breaking all canons of style, Trumper is just himself.'
— ALBERT KNIGHT, *The Complete Cricketer* (1906)

As they would outline in their introduction to *Great Batsmen: Their Methods at a Glance* (1905), George Beldam and C. B. Fry had two related purposes. First was to decode technique, to slow time down so that the action might be better understood:

It has often been said that more may be learnt by watching a good batsman actually playing than by reading all the books that have been written about cricket. But it is impossible to see the details of a stroke as the batsman plays it in real life: the eye cannot follow the rapid and complicated movements of arms, hands and bat. Here Action-Photography is of value since it shows in full detail the various stages in a stroke, and thus betrays secrets which the human eye cannot detect . . . We hazard the prophecy that no one who studies the pictures in this book carefully will fail to acknowledge that they show him a great many points which he never suspected.

The second purpose was subtler but barely less pressing: they aspired to art, or at least to revealing cricket's artistic beauties, to make of batting's physical action something like Watts' 'Physical Action':

> It has been said that the results of instantaneous photography, however true to nature, are generally inartistic in effect: 'very true but very ugly'. Possibly such an opinion may be revised in the light of a study of these pictures of live cricket. Some of the attitudes may seem strange and unfamiliar to those who have never studied great batsmen in action with very close attention. But some of them go to prove how beautiful a game is cricket, and to suggest that the sculptor of modern times might possibly achieve statues of athletic perfection in no wise inferior to those of ancient Greece in the days of the athletic prizemen. Apart from the purely technical aspect of the art of batsmanship in these pages, we hope that the pictures have caught something at any rate of the glow and glory of 'the game with the beautiful name'.

It was clear why Trumper should be foremost among their subjects. Since 1902 he had enhanced his reputation further by top-scoring in the Ashes series of 1903–04. 'The finest batsman in the world,' thought England's captain Pelham Warner. 'Undoubtedly the greatest batsman living and above criticism,' believed Warner's own star batsman R. E. Foster. Perhaps the most resonant summary was that of wicketkeeper Dick Lilley, who stood behind Trumper throughout the batsman's undefeated 185 at the SCG: 'Had he remained to double his score, I should never have tired of watching him.' Trumper's batting transcended national allegiance. Watching him was as exciting to English followers of the game as to Australians – an aesthetic experience to savour, to wonder at, to want to know more of.

No player, not even Grace, not even Ranji, was exciting responses of such widespread lyricism. All manner of interpreters aimed to penetrate the heart of his appeal, the secrets of his success. Even Fry's formidable wife, Beatie, made an attempt, with an unblushing paean in the London periodical *Voice of the Century*:

> There is something peculiarly satisfactory in his having such a suitable name. Victor Trumper, with a real healthy, fresh, pink skin, a long muscular neck, and small, keen, bright eyes. Nothing sad about those eyes, not for one moment. A pair of very fine arms, splendid forearms, wrists, and hands; the whole together makes up a very perfect telephonic communication between his eye and bat. Rather sturdy legs, which never are between the wickets or on the edge of a very wide boundary, but try all day.
>
> When Trumper, chasing the ball, comes towards you, the air seems to divide; he wakes a buzz of power, something like you associate with a very first-rate motor-car. When he bats, if you are fond of cricket in the right sort of way, to you then will Trumper's batting be like reading Robert Louis Stevenson's description of some great granite rocks.

'There they stand, for all the world like their neighbours ashore; only the salt water sobbing between them instead of the quiet earth, and clots of sea-pink blooming on their sides instead of heather; and the great sea-conger to wreathe about the base of them instead of the poisonous viper of the land.'[*]

It is good and pleasant to watch cricket, with the same mind's eye that glories in a beautifully written description. His timing has the exactness, rhythm, and fit of the oceangoing ship's piston-rod – true. Quite naturally his bat hits the ball. Owing to the fibre of the hit a beautiful stroke is the outcome, and this to almost every ball which is bowled. He shifts his feet, steps across, over and back with infinite variety and ease; he can play any bowling on any wicket, not from any particular luck, but just sheer natural ability. He is a poet of cricket; he has a poet's extra sense, touch, and feeling.

Trumper can play, with his bat, a cricket ball as Paganini played his violin; to him it is alive; he plays his strokes by nature, in the easiest possible way, to do it well, and get all there is to be got out of that particular stroke, a note. Trumper is an artist. Some day someone will paint his portrait; it will be hung in a National Portrait Gallery; he will be dressed in white, with his splendid neck bared to the wind, standing on short green grass, against a blue sky; he will be waiting for the ball, the orchestra to strike up. Not even a bowler need go away regretfully from this healthy, strong picture – so easily imagined, a white flannelled knight.

This traverses extraordinary vistas of aesthetic territory – physical, literary, artistic, musical, mechanical. One might even have thought it a bit rich for Australian taste, except that it struck an immediate chord on the other side of the world, being reprinted not only in

---

[*] These lines are from Stevenson's 1882 short story 'The Merry Men'.

Sydney newspapers but in titles as diverse as the *Singleton Argus*, the *Richmond River Express and Tweed Advertiser*, and the *Albury Banner and Wodonga Express*. Farmers in rocking chairs who might never visit a gallery or hear Paganini learned that one of their country-men was scaling similar artistic heights. The Irish-Australian lyric poet Victor Daley, a *Bulletin* favourite, responded with a poem, 'The Great Trumper' (1904), using the penultimate sentence of Beatrice Fry's article as an epigraph:

> 'Trumper is an artist. Some day someone will paint his portrait;
> it will be hung in a National Portrait Gallery; he will be dressed in
> white, with his splendid neck bared to the wind, standing on short
> green grass against a blue sky; he will be waiting for the ball, the
> orchestra to strike up.' – *Mrs. C. B. Fry in an English periodical.*

Ho Statesmen, Patriots, Bards make way!
Your fame has sunk to zero:
For Victor Trumper is to-day
Our one Australian Hero.
High purpose glitters in his eye,
He scorns the filthy dollar;
His splendid neck, says Mrs. Fry,
Is innocent of collar.
He stands upon the short green grass,
Superb, and seems to be now
A nobler young Leonidas
At our Thermopylae now.
Is there not, haply, in the land
Some native-born Murillo
To paint, in colours rich and grand.

This Wielder of the Willow?
Nay, rather let a statue be
Erected his renown to,
That future citizens might see
The gods their sires bowed down to.
Happy the man who while alive
Obtains his meed of glory!
His name for seasons will survive
In fable, song and story.
Evoe Trumper! As for me
It all ends with the moral
That Fame grows on the Willow Tree
And no more on the Laurel.

Daley's mock grandiloquence reveals his satiric purpose – anticipating decades of complaints from Australian artists and writers that all their countrymen care about is sport. There were other poems too, simpler doggerel like Oriel's 'A Bumper to Trumper' (1904) in *The Argus* and E. H. Garnsey's 'Trumper' (1905) in *Athletic News*[*]; in Trumper's honour, Thomas Spencer penned 'The Prerogative of Piper's Flat' (1902), a sequel to his famous comic ballad 'How MacDougall Topped the Score' (1896). Perhaps most ambitiously, Trumper appeared in what would now be regarded as a multimedia project. At the 'Sydney Opera House', then a theatre at the corner of York and King streets, a fine young baritone, George Warsaw, sang a new marching song in

---

[*] Trumper offered the versifier rather limited rhyming possibilities. From Oriel: 'Long life to Victor Trumper,/That record-breaker fine!/I drink it in a bumper/Of clear Australian wine.' From Garnsey: 'The pluck of a hero, a veteran's head,/And modest withal, though his fame it has spread/To the limits of Empire. A bumper!/We'll call it, and take the goodwill for the deed./(He drinks not, nor smokes, let us follow his lead)/Here's health to you, Vic – Victor Trumper.' A couple of years later came Guy Eden's bush ballad 'Victor Trumper'.

praise of 'Australia', whose arrangement featured the use of a bioscope, a form of projector, to display the images of prominent celebrities on a screen. To convey the message of national parity, images of Teddy Roosevelt, Lord Roberts and Lord Kitchener were interspersed with

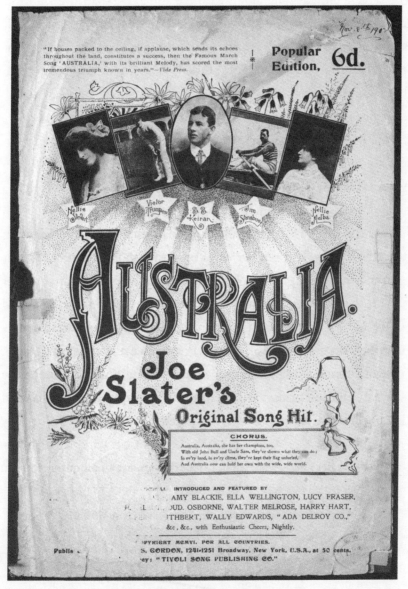

'Australia now can hold her own': Joe Slater's tribute.

those of Melba, her singing rivals Amy Castles and Ada Crossley, actress Nellie Stewart, artist Phil May, swimmer Barney Kieran, and Victor Trumper, against whom cricket-loving composer Joe Slater had played for Leichhardt. When its words appeared on the screen, crowds sang along with the rollicking, patriotic chorus: 'Australia, Australia, she has her champions too/With old John Bull and Uncle Sam, they've shown what they can do;/In ev'ry land, in ev'ry clime, they kept their flag unfurled,/And Australia now can hold her own, with the wide, wide world.' For 15 shillings, the sheet music and slides could be purchased from the Haymarket.

The bulk of the appreciation of Trumper still ran in mainstream cricket circles, but it, too, was of a tone and intimacy unexampled elsewhere. The most startling passages were penned by Albert Knight, a dour professional batsman from unfashionable Leicestershire who played three Tests for England against Trumper in 1903–04. Knight was a Methodist lay preacher who prefaced each innings with a quiet prayer after taking guard, and a cricket writer in a uniquely abstruse vein – the historian Benny Green once joked that some passages in Knight's *The Complete Cricketer* (1906) have yet to be translated. Certainly on the subject of 'the most perfect and accomplished batsman of all time', Knight achieves a pitch of erudition that anticipates Cardus. His description of Trumper at the crease in Sydney has the quality of a religious vision:

A slender figure, wan and drawn of face, cadaverous, but spiritualized with the delicacy of ill health, glides to the wicket. Nor ornament nor colour marked his featureless attire, the personality was all-dominating. He took guard quickly, more quickly took a glance around the field, and received his first ball. 'Dreams of summer dawn in night of rain' presented no fresher vision that this boy's play to that black sea which hid the blistered grass of the Sydney hill. Not in his fascinating collection of strokes, nor in their frank and open execution merely, lay the charm; it was a man playing away a power which was himself rather than in him ... Saint and savage and critic alike 'wondered with a foolish face of praise'. It was a rare and moving sight to look upon that crowd as it rose en masse to watch the ball strike the fence; to see those people standing in hushed expectation ere breaking into unrestrained delight.

There's more – much more. Knight could not write of Trumper without rhapsodising of his spirit, 'so self-forgetful, so manly'. But what's perhaps most noteworthy in the foregoing passage is the waft of mortality into the evolving Trumper legend. Elsewhere Knight would discern in Trumper's batting a 'shadowy gleam of haunting beauty', and a hint of 'where the outlook is infinite'. And while none of his biographers has been able to shed much light on the subject, the visiting Englishmen seem to have been aware that their star opponent was unwell: Warner reported rumours 'going the rounds that Trumper was in bad health'; Foster described Trumper as 'very seedy', and thought he 'did not look at all strong'.

The likeliest explanation is tuberculosis, which claimed a third of Trumper's sisters, three-year-old Elma Claire, in December 1903. After the series, Trumper spent several months 'recuperating' in the Southern Tablelands, at the Bengarralong homestead of a Gundagai pastoralist and racehorse owner, Frederick McEvoy, related by marriage to the journalist J. C. Davis. And while other journalists fussed about the possibility that Trumper might not tour England in 1905, Knight went still further, as though twenty-six-year-old Trumper was as foredoomed as Adonaïs. 'Perchance the statistical expert will yet have many pages to fill with the first-class records of Victor

Trumper,' he wrote. 'Probably not, for such eye and wrist, such light-ning celerity, such risk is for youth alone. Perchance the cold winds of ill-health have already swept across the stream on whose surface lies the glory and the gleam.' And he was, of course, right.*

Cricket fans trying to appraise players of different eras dwell nat-urally on statistics and averages; historians occasionally introduce considerations like the covering of pitches and the sizes of stumps, bats and balls. Invariably overlooked are the basic circumstances of day-to-day living – nutrition, medical care, life expectancy, general levels of prosperity. Trumper is a case in point. Given his proximity to suffer-ers of the disease, he probably carried the *Mycobacterium tuberculosis* most of his life. A great many did. In colonial Australia, tuberculosis had stood at the head of medical causes of death, its symptoms of a chronic cough, fever, weight loss, night sweats and heavy urina-tion familiar to every family. By the early twentieth century, health authorities understood its incidence to be worsened by dense urban living and poor sanitation, but remained in the dark about treating it. In *A New Treatment of Consumption and Other Chronic Chest Diseases* (1904), for example, Duncan Turner recommended lengthy and ener-getic twenty-minute whole-body massages using liberal quantities of cod liver oil, based on an observation by a Scottish doctor of the low incidence of consumption among woollen-mill workers ascribed to their absorption of lanoline through the skin. The commonest prescription was simply a nutritious diet, bed rest and graduated

---

* These passages by Knight were noted in Australia, for they were cited on Trumper's death by an anonymous correspondent in the *Mirror of Australia* on 1 August 1915: 'Knight was a very observant writer, and his reference to Victor "playing away a power" was prophetic. To the writer's mind – and Victor's father is of the same opinion – the deterioration of our late, great batsman's health dated from 1902, when, playing in the wettest season on record in England, Victor scored 2570 runs, and made eleven centuries. The exertions of that tour, followed by another strenuous season in Australia, undermined his health, and he never fully recovered.'

exercise preferably in a country location, such as Trumper undertook.

The *Gundagai Times*, naturally, welcomed the celebrity convalescent, not least for confirming the local reputation for healthfulness: 'His decision to seek a restoration to good health here is a wise one, for the climate of Gundagai taken all round is not to be eclipsed in any part of the state, as our health record proves.' And despite his ailments, Trumper reciprocated the local hospitality by turning out for Gundagai against Gobarralong: a huge crowd converged to watch 'the champion batsman of the world' play a whirlwind innings before contributing to local folklore by getting out to a railway worker from Cootamundra, Jack Harrold. Twenty years later, the *Gundagai Times* was still introducing Harrold as 'the man who bowled Victor Trumper'. Forty years later, an aspiring writer working with the Australian Department of Information based a short story on his father's recollection of Trumper visiting Gundagai: 'When Trumper Went to Billabong' (1944) by Dal Stivens, whom we shall meet more fully in Chapter 10, appeared in the popular weekly *John O'London's*. And while nobody knows for sure, it's not unlikely that the cricket-loving Bradman family of Yeo Yeo named their first son for the visiting divinity: Victor Bradman, elder brother to Donald, was born later in 1904.

Here in Trumper's time may have lain another reason for Beldam and Fry to set out to document him – that there was a sense of Trumper passing before the world. None could have known that he had a meagre decade to live. But perhaps his chroniclers intuited a special urgency about capturing Trumper for visual posterity. The 'portrait' Beatie Fry thought necessary could not wait until 'some day': it was an instant necessity, best suited to an instantaneous medium.

•

Trumper returned to England midst great enthusiasm. He was introduced to the Prince of Wales; he was invited to pose for a wax likeness by Madame Tussauds; he contributed that lengthy article to *Fry's Magazine* described in Chapter 2; he agreed to write cricket columns for the *Daily Chronicle*. Then, mysteriously, he didn't.

The custom among English amateurs of supplementing their income by writing for the press, established by Ranji and Fry, was now well entrenched. The sheer volume of articles by the likes of Warner, MacLaren and Jessop were the subject of some jocularity, as in lines penned the previous year for the *Evening News*.

> Oh, what will become of our national cricket
> When every player devotes
> The time he would otherwise spend at the wicket
> To penning elaborate notes?
>
> To face a fast bowler is always exciting.
> But wouldn't it cause you distress,
> If between each two overs you had to be writing
> Your views on the game for the press!

Trumper, an Australian, would have made an exotic addition to these ranks: as the *Chronicle* introduced him in an excited promotion of his forthcoming appearance, he was 'admittedly the finest batsman to visit this country'. But Australians, thinking them a source of needless friction, had remained averse to such forays into journalism. By signing a contract with the *Chronicle*, in fact, Trumper had placed himself in breach of a tour agreement he knew well enough to have quoted to Worcestershire's Paul Foley three years earlier. 'No member of the team shall correspond for any newspaper by letter or cable or otherwise during the tour,' read the relevant section. 'A breach of this clause renders the culprit liable to a fine of £100.' Its application must have been promptly brought to Trumper's attention. The day after his first scheduled column failed to appear, the *Chronicle* explained its absence by a letter of apology from the man himself.

> Dear sir – I regret that owing to a prohibition put on all members of the Australian team – a restriction which, unfortunately, I misinterpreted – I am prevented from carrying out the contract I made with you last week to write daily cricket notes in your paper. Trusting that this explanation will be accepted by your readers and yourselves, and that you are satisfied with my good faith in the matter.

What exactly happened here? Did Trumper fancy taking advantage of the same opportunities as were dangled before English amateurs such as MacLaren, also a *Chronicle* contributor? Was he pushing commercial boundaries, on the timeless principle that careers are short but life is long? After all, by now he had opened his sports store with one teammate, Hanson Carter, and married the sister of another, Jim Kelly; she, Annie, was actually on the tour, pregnant with their daughter. The only hint is contained in a single paragraph deep in *An Australian Cricketer on Tour* (1905), the travelogue published by their player-manager, the 'inveterate snapshotter' Frank Laver. Decrying the writing on cricket by English amateurs as 'being questionable in the interests of the game for it to continue' and outlining the Australian fine system, Laver reported: 'The proprietors of one newspaper were so anxious to get articles on the game by one of our members that they offered to pay his amount [£100] if one fine would cover a series of articles by that member.' As that member was almost certainly Trumper, one must presume that the *Chronicle* offered to pay the fine if it was a one-off, then perhaps baulked at the idea of covering it every time he wrote.

Like his flirtations with English counties in 1902, Trumper's dalliance with the *Chronicle* in 1905 is one of those oddities his biographers have sidestepped, perhaps because it scarcely reconciles with his reputation for a saintly scorn of 'the filthy dollar'. But Trumper appears guilty of naivety at least, caught up in mass media manoeuverings for celebrity and sensation. With this he and his teammates had a further brush when they stepped forth for their first practice session in the Nursery at Lord's on the morning of 1 May, and were surrounded by no fewer than twenty-four photographers massed to take team photographs, plus a newsreel cameraman from Edison Kinetoscope to film them doing so. The Australians were caught slightly off guard as they gathered in their usual hearty manner – on seeing the newsreel later at the Palace Theatre, they were amused at the vigorous V-signs that Laver exchanged with fellow Victorian Warwick Armstrong, and by spinner Bill Howell rolling a ball off Trumper's capped head. They were less impressed by the importunings of the photographers, whom Laver regarded as 'a perfect nuisance.'

> We required from each a guarantee that he would give each member of the team a copy and would not use the photo in any form whatever for advertising purposes on postcards. Some avoided the latter condition rather cleverly, making cards the same size and shape as ordinary postcards and selling them. With all our care it did not prevent postcards from being issued. Some of these were faked and frightful productions, heads were stuck on bodies of other people &c. The pictures on one postcard did not in the

least degree look like us. The publishers did not even trouble to put moustaches on faces where moustaches should have been.

Now, it's arguable, Laver was being the naive one. The money in cricket no longer came and went only via the gate. It underpinned other commercial objectives, leveraged from feat, name and image: if the Australians declined to make it themselves, it would be made from them. Nor need this always be crass or exploitative, and other ends were achievable. The visitors probably felt a certain reassurance when out of the ruck of photographers at Lord's that day stepped a figure they knew, liked and trusted.

•

Uniquely among Beldam's numerous 'sittings', this session with his Australian subjects is actually dated, in the diary of his artist friend Henry Tuke, who with his other artist friend Albert Chevallier Tayler were helpmates in the work. Beldam turned thirty-seven that 1 May, and had plans to celebrate his birthday later at a Royal Academy dinner. First, though, his purpose was to obtain photographs of Trumper and two teammates, Clem Hill and Algy Gehrs. The spring weather threw down a damp and blustery challenge, but the painters patiently anchored the camera as Beldam showed off a new trick, evolved over the past year, of bowling the ball with his right hand and taking the photograph with his left by means of a pneumatic push connected to the Videx by a twenty-metre cord. There was none of the larkishness of the morning. Three years earlier, Trumper had smiled at the novelty of being photographed; now, having first stood still in his stance then allowed his grip to be closely examined, he produced hooks, pulls, cuts and drives on

A day at Lord's: Trumper at a glance.

request, as Beldam strove to facilitate with sympathetic deliveries. On at least one occasion, perhaps when the ball was unsuitable, he was bowled.

The Australians and Beldam were to see a great deal of each other in this summer. Three days later, as the tour commenced formally at Crystal Palace, the photographer turned back into a cricketer and bowled to them in an actual match, representing a Gentlemen of England XI led by Grace, and also including Fry, MacLaren, Warner, Jessop and Poidevin. Now Beldam actually hit Trumper's stumps for real, to the disappointment of an expectant crowd. Had he detected some semblance of weakness from his photographic studies? After all, by agreeing to be frozen in time, Beldam's subjects were revealing aspects of their game previously imperceptible; they were consenting to their demystification.

Yet the mutual intrigue must have been strong. Photographer and subject could regard themselves as involved in parallel pursuits. 'Shot', 'catch', 'timing': these were words as meaningful in the use of a camera as of a cricket bat. The secret of his success, Beldam thought, lay in his being a cricketer himself, which put him 'in touch with the mind and movements of the player'.

A foreign pupil once thought it was the 'leetle' brush which caused the master to do such beautiful water-colour work. The master gave him the brush, and he came back with the remark that it was not the 'leetle' brush but the hand behind it, and his master ventured to suggest that there might also be something behind the hand. So in Action-Photography, given the right kind of camera, everything must depend on the timing powers and perception of the artist; and these must be also combined with good knowledge of the principles of cricket, golf, lawn tennis, or any other game of which photographs are required.

The surroundings, possibly the crowd, everything which is likely to distract the attention of the operator must be obliterated, and a kind of telepathy must exist between the player and the camera artist.

When Beldam next photographed Trumper, there were just such surroundings, and a 'kind of telepathy' very much at work.

·

To continue his study, Beldam now pursued Trumper to The Oval. Exactly when went unrecorded, but it was almost certainly before play on a day of Australia's game against Surrey, which spanned 11–13 May 1905. We know Beldam was present because the *Illustrated Sporting and Dramatic News* the following week published a photograph of Beldam in street attire standing at cover with his camera while Clem Hill played to leg on a pitch marked at the eastern edge of the square – from this can be inferred the services of a bowler. We know also that the game had a noon start with no tea break, and the

The photographer photographed: Beldam at The Oval.

shortish shadows in the photographs Beldam took of Trumper are consistent with their being taken in late morning.

The Oval was a location pregnant with meaning: the venue where Australians had made a fortune in 1878, lost a great Test in 1880, and won a great Test in 1882; the home of one of the county clubs that had recently sought to recruit Trumper. It was also a vision of the future of cricket watching, served as it was by the world's first electric tube and a brand new tram line, surmounted by a superb pavilion hosting 400 000 visitors a year. Overshadowed by the gasholders of the South Metropolitan Gas Works, increasingly encircled by factories, foundries and breweries, The Oval's playing expanse now had a *rus in urbe* quality, a remnant of the days when Kennington had been open fields and market gardens.

With the King as patron and the Lord Chief Justice as president, Surrey County CC was at a zenith of self-estimation. Secretary Charles Alcock had just published a sumptuous history billing the county as 'the Cradle of Cricket', dismissing the traditional claims to that title of the village of Hambledon, and also subtly puncturing the pretensions of Marylebone. Socially exclusive Lord's might headquarter cricket's high councils, believed Alcock, but The Oval was the ground of the people, providing 'a great education for them in every possible way'. In a verse in *Fry's Magazine*, the Surrey amateur Digby Jephson saluted the diversity of Oval crowds:

> There are soldiers, sailors and postmen there,
> There are clerks from their high-backed stools.
> There are tinkers, tailors and booing brats,
> And swells of The City in silken hats
> And men from the clubs in immaculate spats
> But all of them know the rules.

Their own rules were an attendance to pleasure of utmost seriousness and decorum. In the *Jubilee Book*, Ranji had reported the astonishment of a German visiting a county match at The Oval at 'the extreme orderliness of the many thousands' in the presence of a mere 'five policemen' when 'abroad it would require at least 300 policemen to keep such a large crowd in order'. When Neville Cardus later argued for cricket as the 'national art' of a people 'prone to be ashamed of living the life aesthetic', he gestured not towards St John's Wood but Kennington: 'Go among the shilling crowd any fine day at The Oval and what do you hear? Little technical jargon, little talk of offbreaks and the position of the left funny bone in the late cut. Instead you will hear many delighted cries of "Beautiful stroke – Beautiful!"'

That day at The Oval, Beldam was pursuing his own 'beautiful stroke'. His photographs at Lord's had been of different shots from more or less similar angles, just either side of straight. Now he sought the perfect encapsulation of the perfect drive down the ground. Peering down through the grid of his viewfinder, he worked his way around a 180-degree arc, stopping to take pictures at five points between mid-on and second slip, in the process exposing a background panorama of the ground: low-level terraces fringed by distant houses; the exoskeleton of the gasometers; the silhouette of a solitary tree beside the pavilion's solemn bulk. The passage of time can be sensed from the lesser and greater concentrations of onlookers, presumably building up as game time approached. In some images, smudged figures appear on the outfield, including a woman with a parasol, perhaps Annie Trumper.

A recurrent detail is noticeable: Trumper's front foot poised in midair as the bat flourished at the top of its swing, inspired perhaps by Beldam's successful picture of Ranji the previous year, as if to stress the subject's balance and light-footedness, and also the instantaneity

A day at The Oval: Trumper's foot hovers.

of the medium. In no other photographic sequence of Beldam's would this prove such a motif – there is a sense of him exploring his camera's limits as he documented Trumper's. When Beldam moved to point, side-on to the action, he paused with special care. This time, he wanted Trumper to commence his stride from outside the crease, his back foot a metre ahead of the line, a preliminary step to this position assumed – the straight drive potentiated, attack sharpened to a fine point. To capture it, he planned a photograph of equivalent skill and nerve, tilting the plate holder at the back of the Videx so as to produce images of a landscape rather than a portrait shape. This was something he very seldom did. In the rest of his oeuvre there are only a handful of none-too-successful attempts to work in such a way. Such a photograph required the leaving of a space for an on-rushing cricketer to fill – it risked a wasted plate, which Beldam deplored. It was a gesture of confidence in his subject, that Trumper had the athleticism to match the conception. It's also possible Beldam looked at the background, for from his sideways vantage was visible a gulf in the skyline opened by the width of Clayton Street stretching away from the ground – defined on the left by a boarding house and on the right by the Clayton Arms Hotel, it was in its way the perfect frame, especially in a photograph now absent the orienting presence of stumps.

The publican of the Clayton Arms, one Frederick Brooke, had shown a shrewd understanding of the conspicuousness of his establishment and allowed advertisers to emblazon its facade: a big banner spruiked *Sporting Life* ('The Paper the Professionals Read'); smaller ones promoted Rosbach ('Empress of Table Waters'), Bovril ('Bovril Always Scores') and Claymore Whisky ('Tired Nature's Sweet Restorer'). But Beldam blurred these, and also the legend 'Refreshments' on the front of The Oval's bar, by widening his aperture and shrinking his depth of field. A crowd had collected square of the wicket – all those soldiers and sailors, tinkers and tailors, orderly and dark-clad. With the twiddling of a knob, they too became an indistinct mass. Trumper would be the image's entire foreground in a narrow strip of focus.

There survives no contact sheet or diary note chronicling the order or even the number of photographs Beldam took of Trumper's spring from this angle. All we know is that three images survive. One he would save for his later small book *Cricket Illustrated* (1908). It was almost but not quite right. Trumper was *just* short of occupying the Clayton Street gap; his left wrist was bent *just* a little awkwardly; his weight had not *quite* fully transferred; two dark figures, perhaps police constables, loitered in the middle distance.[*]

Variation on a theme: Trumper drives.

---

[*]     In his personal copy of *Cricket Illustrated*, now owned by collector John Hawkins, Beldam annotated the image for comparison with a photo on the adjacent page of W. G. Grace, using his favoured technical jargon: 'Well marked left arm screw but wrist joint bent (how unfortunate!). Right hand relaxed (not revolved). Symptoms cf opposite page reversed, bat face looking backward and not straight at you (due to left wrist joint) etc etc.'

It has the hallmarks of a first attempt, after which Beldam moved ever so slightly left, so that Trumper's head in his normal stance would have reposed between the distant ogee-roofed towers of the board school on Kennington Road.

Beldam's method was almost always to collect an image of the stroke in completed form, so he had Trumper proceed all the way to the follow-through, the bat having described more than a full circle, shoulders now completely turned. This time the framing worked better, for Trumper stopped just short of the right side of the gulf, almost vertically upright, eyes seemingly fixed on the disappearing ball. Beldam would have withdrawn the plate with a feeling of confidence. But could he get Trumper at the extent of his spring?

For Beldam, photography was often a rush, a compromise, seeking opportune moments when subjects were willing and the climate was favourable. Photography remained so novel that few had a clear idea how long it took. Beldam enjoyed relating a story of seeking permission to photograph the players at a certain county club, and the secretary asking the duration of exposures. 'A thousandth of a second,' said Beldam. 'Oh well, then,' the secretary replied. 'You'll soon be through with our eleven – about one one-hundredth of a second for the whole team.'

The build-up of the crowd visible through his viewfinder would have told Beldam now that time was running out. One can imagine ground staff, officials and policemen looking at their watches wondering when all this palaver would be done; one can imagine spectators looking on from afar bemused by the stop-start action; one can imagine the ball leaving the bowler's hand, the batsman commencing to leap, and the photographer clicking to release the mirror, engage the shutter, expose the plate, and wonder . . . *had he got it?*

# 6

## 'HE HAS NO STYLE, YET HE IS ALL STYLE'

'London, an Edwardian summer's day. George Beldam,
cricket's photographic pioneer, captures the essence of Victor Trumper
in a picture that has become an Australian icon.'
– Caption in *Wisden Cricketers' Almanack*, 2000

On 1 August 1905, Swan Electric Engraving Company, a West End firm specialising in art prints, made available an unusual item: a limited edition India proof photogravure, 14½" × 16½ in" (37 cm × 42 cm), of a cricketer in the act of jumping out to drive. The cricketer with that look; the cricketer who had to be seen; the cricketer whose strokes, in Philip Trevor's words, were beyond 'the ordinary eye to follow'; now, at least in theory, the sight of Victor Trumper's batting was available to all. And it was merely a foretaste. Three weeks later, Macmillan & Co. formally released *Great Batsmen: Their Methods at a Glance*, its 716 pages featuring '600 Action-Photographs' by 'George W. Beldam' and a text by 'Charles B. Fry'.

For a decade, cricket's benchmark pictorial work had been Alcock's stately *Great Cricketers and Cricket Grounds*, with its portraits, poses and panoramas. Now Beldam offered imperious drives, rasping cuts, fearless hooks, scintillating glances, lavish backlifts, flourishing follow-throughs – the accent throughout was on attack, and off the front foot. All were adorned with Fry's mandarin prose, pronouncing voluminously on 'wristwork', 'armswing' and 'shoulder turn', insisting on 'correct bodily mechanism' and the 'left-shoulder-forward principle', distinguishing sharply between 'upward forward swing' and 'downward flicking turn', between 'wrist leverage' and 'finger manipulation'.

Fry had arrived at length on criteria of batting style – that of minimal effort to maximum effect, and that of a tasteful orthodoxy that nonetheless did not impinge on individuality. He had discerned these in Ranjitsinhji those years ago; now they appealed to him as ideals to aspire to, as an index of batting's refinement. The structure of *Great Batsmen* told a tale of progress. Grace, as ever, was accorded pride of place in the 'Individualities' section, with twenty-six photographs, although with a note of apology for his proconsular bulk, stiff arms and heavy boots. 'What a pity Action-Photography was not invented twenty years ago!' exclaimed the authors, as if to ward off complaints of awkwardness.

Second in line of descent came twenty photographs of Ranji, wrists as supple as Grace's were unyielding. Third came no fewer than thirty-three photographs of Trumper, more than for any other cricketer, perhaps because none so completely fulfilled the co-authors' twin purposes of providing instruction and also aesthetic example. His slim physique bent this way and that; his strokes streaked away to every degree of the field; in the photograph being marketed by Swan Engraving, which in *Great Batsmen* became 'Plate XXVII', Trumper managed both to surge towards the future and to hark back to models of antiquity, in his classical proportions, broad shoulders tapering to the waist, and taut, dynamic muscularity. The image's antecedents, in fact, were as sculptural as pictorial, specifically the classics of *contrapposto* – the posing of a figure with weight unevenly distributed, one leg 'engaged', the other leg 'free'. Impetus for *contrapposto* had come from the desire to capture ideal male athletic form. Here was a modern culmination of that exercise, loaded with asymmetries: one foot grounded, the other airborne; one hand gloved, the other bare; the shirt both loose and tight; the arms both gloriously free and tensed for action. For all Trumper's evident agility, his position had a curious aerodynamic stability, controlled by the level, unblinking eyes, fit for plinth as well as pitch. And against the murkily dark backdrop, the batsman's flannels had a marble whiteness; the folds could have been worked by a riffler.

Fry followed Trumper, with practised modesty, then a procession of style's various interpreters in subtle alternation, of Australians and Englishman, amateur and professional. It's when the 'Strokes Illustrated' section is added that the mix can be seen as appreciably skewed. Sixty-five amateurs are sprinkled with only nineteen professionals – batting's example, the co-authors clearly agreed, could only be set by cricket's aristocracy.

Among that cognoscenti, *Great Batsmen* was understood at once to be a landmark publication. Copies were presented to the King, to the Prince of Wales, and to Surrey CCC, among whose members advertising leaflets were circulated. *Cricket* offered a prospectus. Swan Engraving released two further photogravures, of prancing

Ranji and seigneurial F. S. Jackson, to complement the Trumper.[*]
Critical acclaim was unanimous. 'The best book about England's game

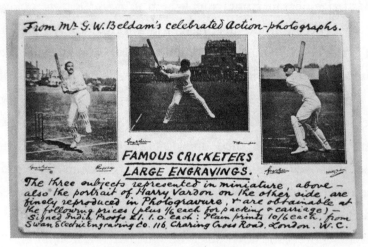

From Mr G. W. Beldam's celebrated action-photographs.

FAMOUS CRICKETERS
LARGE ENGRAVINGS.

The three subjects represented in miniature, above –
also the portrait of Harry Vardon on the other side, are
finely reproduced in Photogravure, & are obtainable at
the following prices (plus 1/6 each for packing & carriage) –
Signed India Proofs £1. 1. 0. each : Plain prints 10/6 each, from
Swan Electric Engraving Co. 116, Charing Cross Road, London. W. C.

Icons in the making: yours for a guinea.

yet published': *Evening News*. 'The most precious gem that cricket literature has ever possessed': *Sporting Life*. Here, explained *The Graphic*,
was a whole new way of approaching the game. Hitherto it had been
impossible 'to see the details of a stroke, so momentary [was] every
movement'. At last, with this 'very large number of photographs of
famous batsmen in action', one could 'study at leisure the most minute
details of their methods'. For critics' abstractions had been substituted
the camera's artless truthfulness: 'Every one of the six hundred photographs is an actuality. If the proverb is true about an ounce of fact and a
pound of theory, the book ought to be invaluable.' Classical criteria of
beauty, moreover, had been met, claimed the *Illustrated London News*:

> Sometimes the pose in which the batsman has been caught is
> ungraceful, even awkward; on the other hand we are inclined

---

[*] Swan made available 500 India proofs – a fine, very smooth paper, designed to
show off every small detail – of each image at a guinea each. There was also an
unspecified number of plain prints at 10s 6d.

to think that had our national game been known to the ancient Greeks, their sculptors must have discovered on the cricket-ground suggestions for statues of athletes equal in grace and vigour to any inspired by the Olympic Games.

Thank you, Victor Trumper.

•

Cricket and art: the intersection exercised Beldam ever more, so much that he had been working secretly with another collaborator. His friend Albert Chevallier Tayler was at peak renown as a portrait and genre painter, recently acclaimed for 'The Ceremony of the Garter' (1901) and 'Five Kings' (1903); he was also a cricket devotee, appearing regularly for the Artists XI (Hillyard Swinstead, Reginald Blomfield, G. Spencer Watson) against the Authors XI (E. V. Lucas, P. G. Wodehouse, Arthur Conan Doyle, E. W. Hornung). Now, just as Hal Ludlow had turned Beldam's Harry Vardon into a statue, Tayler agreed to produce pastel drawings of leading players based on Beldam photographs. Over summer the forty-eight prints in *The Empire's Cricketers* were exhibited in batches of four at the New Bond Street Gallery, marketed as folio-size lithographs by the Fine Art Society, and finally collected by Dawbarn & Ward in a cloth-bound portfolio: thirty-seven Englishmen and eleven Australians, pristine in white against grey-green backgrounds, splashed with colour by their caps and waistbands.

Art inspired by sport derived from photography? It was a doubly bold notion, and the co-venturers seem to have known it, for Tayler's catalogue downplayed his debt to the camera, merely acknowledging Beldam's 'information and assistance'. Nor was the response better than lukewarm. The *Illustrated London News*'s reviewer, 'W.M.', thought that the 'complex excellence of this or that action' would be 'lost on those who are not keen followers of the game'. But those keen followers, increasingly accustomed by photography to exact likenesses and fine detail, weren't impressed either, troubled by touches like artistic blurrings and contoured hatching. *Cricket*'s perennial editor Charles Alcock, in this context an important arbiter of taste, regarded the drawings with particular disfavour. The average cricketer, he thought, 'may want to know why Dr Grace looks five feet high, and why he wears boots without laces; why Pelham Warner uses a bat which is not spliced, and why he is also without laces to his boots; why Rhodes has a deformed right hand and why he is bowling a ball which would be discarded, even in a preparatory school, as much too small'; not to mention 'why all the cricketers wear shirts with stripes running in all sorts of curious ways – he is hardly likely to be satisfied with being told that the stripes are really shadows, for he will say that he never sees a cricketer wear shadows in that way'. From photographs Alcock could accept angularities and oddities; from art he expected . . . well, art.*

Yet Alcock had a point. From Beldam's portfolio, possibly because he was straining to avoid too obvious a reliance on the photographs, Tayler chose rather less than compelling examples, muting the effect of his images: sales duly fell short of expectations, and a further forty-two drawings were never released. Where *The Empire's Cricketers* did enjoy a curious afterlife was in Melbourne the following year, local tobacco manufacturers Sniders & Abrahams reproducing forty of the drawings as cards for their 'Milo' cigarettes – unusual cigarette cards for not relying on regulation portraits, and a foretaste of the promiscuous uses to which Beldam photographs would later be put.

---

* If the co-venturers were disappointed, they might have consoled themselves with an idea they were ahead of their time: nine of the prints have since found their way into Britain's National Portrait Gallery, alongside only one other work by Tayler.

The Empire's cigarette: Tayler's Trumper as print and card.

*Great Batsmen* itself had by then made the journey to Australia, and been received as favourably as it had in England. 'Even in these days of marvellous productions and reproductions it is scarcely possible for the work of the photo-author-cricketers to be excelled': *The Argus*. 'No cricketer should fail to see it, while batsmen who aspire to distinction should study it': *The Queenslander*. 'Not all the theory in the world from the pen of the best writer could convey to the mind the full idea of how to make a stroke or bowl a ball in the same convincing manner as that supplied by the art of photography': the *Sydney Mail*. Which pointed up a subtle tension. 'Mr. Fry has very high praise for our own Victor Trumper's style,' reported *The Australasian*, 'and certainly the attitude and poise of the incomparable New South Wales batsman are so graceful in making certain strokes that they would serve admirably as a model for a cricket sculptor.' Yet in the presence of the finest image, it was noticeable that Fry had virtually nothing to say.

•

Trumper enthralled both collaborators, but on them he appears to have had quite different effects. Of no other individual batsman did Beldam include more images; to no images did Fry add less. Fry seems to have found the Australian slightly perplexing. 'Victor Trumper is, perhaps, the most difficult batsman in the world to reduce to words,' he began his succinct appreciation. 'He has no style, and yet he is all style. He has no fixed canonical method of play, he defies all the orthodox rules, yet every stroke he plays satisfies the ultimate criterion of style – minimum of effort, maximum of effect.' By this last observation Fry accommodated Trumper in his aesthetic convictions. But to Beldam's most exquisite image, he could add only a sixteen-word caption: 'Jumping out for a straight drive. Shoulders, arms, and wrists will all come into the stroke.'

This terseness stood out because Fry was otherwise so prolix, capable of spending whole pages on individual stances and grips, and of distinctions of an almost inconceivable fineness.* By now he was almost prepared to accept the visual as the preferable form of immediate testimony: 'The truth is that the action of any stroke is very complicated, and impossible to describe completely and accurately

---

\* As an example, Fry explaining the difference between a 'drive' and a 'push':

'It is almost impossible to distinguish between a stroke which is a genuine outright drive and one which is played with a modified swing scarcely amounting to more than a forward push. If there is any swing at all in the stroke, as distinguished from thrust, the stroke immediately differs in kind from the genuine forward stroke played only with a thrusting action of the right arm, aided perhaps by the wrists. But as some players manage to play this push-stroke in a very lively manner, and as others drive with a very short and modified swing, and as the foot-work in both these strokes is often precisely similar, it is very difficult to distinguish between the two strokes. When a batsman either runs or jumps out to the ball, or when he moves his left foot to the ball with a very short step and hits with a pronounced swing, the custom is to call the stroke a drive. But when a player reaches out at the ball with one long stride of the left foot, just as in playing the push-stroke, and swings at the ball, the stroke is sometimes called a forward stroke and sometimes a drive . . .'

in words . . . The actual movements in a stroke can be portrayed only by a series of instantaneous photographs.' But the concession did not come easily, partly because any image that 'spoke for itself' left the critic such as Fry uneasily placed – as Walter Benjamin would observe, the circulation of mechanically reproduced images subverted the former circles of privileged interpretation by rendering every consumer a 'semi-expert'. It may not be coincidental that Fry's writing on cricket technique after *Great Batsmen*, mainly in disquisitions for his magazine, grew ever longer and more complicated, to the point where he confessed a fear of growing 'too abstruse to be intelligible' and of indulging in 'unblushing theoreticalness'. Abandoning references to 'the sculptor of modern times', he began exhorting batsmen to behave as 'a live machine, a system of levers whose action in each case must be perfectly adjusted in order to produce the perfect stroke': the images in Fry's solo treatise *Batsmanship* (1912) are staid and inert. Fry's 1939 autobiography then mysteriously omitted Beldam altogether, in favour of, among other things, an account of his 1934 meeting with Hitler and sympathy with Nazism.

Trumper's influence on Beldam was quite otherwise. He also had to 'reduce' the Australian, from a moving three-dimensional subject to a stationary two-dimensional object. But for the first time in sporting history he demonstrated how skilfully and memorably this could be done. At a time when sport and photography were barely acquainted, he integrated them like extensions of the other. 'Jumping Out' represents an incunabula, a first tracing, of the modern action photograph, anticipating its whole grammar of athletic motion and of mass spectacle. Aspects of its memorability go to the essence not just of cricket but of image making itself.

•

At the simplest level, 'Jumping Out' is black and white, with all the shades between: the pale cream of Trumper's attire standing out against the inkiness of the terraces, the dark line of the buildings against the grey luminosity of the sky. It is thereby rendered at once historic and classic, fitting into the tradition of serious photography that scorned colour film long after it became freely available – 'black and white *are* the colours of photography', decreed Robert Frank famously. 'Jumping Out' has been 'colourised' at various times since, but always at a cost to its sensitivity of detail and nuances of mood, its roundness, volume and depth. For where black-and-white tends to date cinema and television, we seem to read black-and-white photographs in a different way. As the noted British colorimetrist David Wright put it: 'You may get closer to reality with colour, but the closer you get the more obvious it becomes that the picture is not a real thing.'

Beldam also freshens a relatively familiar action by a novel vantage. The stroke is both instantly recognisable as the platonic ideal of a straight drive, returning the ball from whence it came, and uniquely Trumper's: this is the way to play it, yet only *this* batsman can play it *this* way. Trumper hurtles headlong across the frame, insouciantly out of his ground, taking what's implied is a second stride towards the ball, the safety of the crease far behind. There is no hedging, no half-measure – Trumper is daring all on the basis of his skill, eye, and also, in some measure, his amateur status, ambiguous and disputed as it sometimes was.

To Beldam's photograph, in fact, there is actually a curious counterpart. Two years earlier, Hurst and Blackett had published an instruction manual, *The Cricket of Abel, Hirst and Shrewsbury* (1903), featuring thirty-four photographs of the so-named professionals, Abel, Shrewsbury and George Hirst. The author, E. F. Benson, is remembered today for a sequence of comic novels, the Mapp and Lucia series, and for membership of a gifted family – an older sister was a trailblazing Egyptologist; an older brother wrote the words to 'Land of Hope and Glory'. His role as instructor in this case was based on the eccentric premise that as himself a poor cricketer he was better equipped as a teacher: 'On the principle of "Set a thief to catch a thief", a duffer has here been set to catch a duffer, while at the same time the whole teaching is, I hope, strictly according to the actual play of good players, as shown by observation, by photographs.'

Except that from Edgar Basebe's photographs could be deduced almost nothing: the subjects stood solemnly and stonily still. To illustrate 'running out to drive', Basebe positioned Abel in the same place at the same ground against the same backdrop as Beldam positioned Trumper for a more or less identical stroke. Yet the differences are so marked that the latter could almost be a comment on the former. Abel's sole semblance of animation is a slightly raised back heel; Trumper appears as if taking wing. Abel's hands are cautiously parted; Trumper's act in harmonious concert. Abel is anchored by the stumps and a heavily criss-crossed crease; Trumper is alone but for a fraction of a crease line falling irrelevantly away. There is nobody to watch Abel; Trumper is the cynosure of all eyes. Between them, the photographs form a world view. Abel, the archetypal professional, is ultimately a drudge with an eye to his livelihood; Trumper, an amateur at least for the sake of this argument, is the free spirit at play. Only one has the dash, the *élan*, to inspire and lead. It's worth noting, too, that Abel, despite having accumulated more than 20 000 first-class runs in the previous decade, was granted but a single small photograph in *Great Batsmen*; Arthur Shrewsbury, having gloomily taken his own life not long before in fear of a suspected illness, did not appear at all.

If that social demarcation is no longer significant to a modern audience, the sense of expansiveness, abandon and even innocence remains. The shot is all instinct, no calculation. The backlift is high, thrillingly high, and straight, pendulously straight; the high grip reveals most of the handle; the protective gear is light, the clothing unmarred by logos or brands. The contrast is now, perhaps, between Trumper's unsullied whiteness and the encroachments of commerce, symbolised in the brand names looming indistinctly in the background, in anticipation of the role of sponsors, broadcasters and other corporates in sport's diffusion. Trumper is holding aloof from them, his absorption in his task reinforced by the photograph's perspective. His face is in profile – physiognomically distinctive, inherently fleeting. The profile is the way we would see passers-by if we turned sideways in the street, the view we have when invisible to another person, the underpinning of the silhouette, the mug shot and the regal outline on coinage. Around the turn of the century it was also enjoying a quiet vogue. Aubrey Beardsley had turned languidly side-on to Frederic Evans; Rodin had stood out in relief against the backdrop of his alter ego, 'The Thinker', for Edward Steichen; Virginia Woolf had accentuated her melancholy beauty by looking away from G. C. Beresford. Trumper's spontaneous profile now seems differently expressive, enacting big sport's performative relations: as he is appraised, appreciated and consumed, he has eyes only for the ball.

Trumper's quickness, meanwhile, is conveyed by the picture's tiny tincture of imperfection. With only a thousandth of a second to play with, the Videx has done its best. Batspeed sometimes confounded Beldam: the nearer the bat to an approaching ball, the likelier it would be bowed or blurred on the print; from one Beldam photograph of Frank Ford, the bat is missing altogether. Not here: in the top left of 'Jumping Out', Trumper's bat is not only captured at the point of perfect stillness before commencing its downswing, but slightly tilted to pronounce its wandlike slimness. The background verticals of the three little chimney pots and the horizontals of The Oval terraces narrate the bat's imminent passage down and through the plane of the ball; the open sky in the top right suggests an exit point for the stroke. But in the lower right, Trumper's forward-flung front foot is ever-so-slightly blurred.

The effect is accidental: the cause is the focal-plane shutter's transit, exposing the right-hand side of the plate ever so slightly longer than the left. It's also predictive of the role distortion would play in the photographic documentation of sport, beginning with the very first outstanding vision of motor racing, Jacques-Henri Lartigue's 'Grand prix de l'ACF' (1912), in which the body of a Schneider automobile is sharply defined but its wheels cartoonishly elongated. Later on such effects would be deliberately sought after, most famously by *Sports Illustrated*'s John Zimmerman in his images of the basketballer Tiny Archibald (1958 and 1971), and the pitchers Vida Blue (1971) and Nolan Ryan (1973). In 'Jumping Out', it is more a case of nature defying technology: Trumper meets the machine, and transcends it.

Another effect in *Great Batsmen* seems perfectly deliberate: Beldam's placement, as Plate XXVIII, immediately following 'Jumping Out', of his photograph of Trumper's follow-through. By compelling their consecutive reading, he lends the images a cinematic quality. Since the Australians had filed past the British Mutoscope camera in 1899, there had been other gestures to recording cricket as a moving image. In 1901, Fry and Ranji had played half a dozen hasty strokes for a home motion-picture device called a Kinora; that same year, the newsreel makers Mitchell & Kenyon had filmed Lancashire's controversial fast bowler, Arthur Mold, in the nets at Old Trafford after he had been no-balled for throwing in a county match; from 1905 footage survives of the Australians in the field at Trent Bridge and going through stilted motions in the Nursery at Lord's. In juxtaposing the start and finish of a straight drive, Beldam foretells the precedence of the moving image in sport.

It was a mode in which Beldam continued experimenting. For *Great Bowlers and Fielders* (1906), he linked no fewer than seven plates of his Middlesex teammate J. T. Hearne for a complete 'pictorial analysis' of successive stages of his action; for Wallis Myers' *The Complete Lawn Tennis Player* (1908), he assembled two sequences of the Australian Norman Brookes demonstrating the American service; for *Fry's Magazine* in 1909 he put together a ten-shot 'cinematographoid' of Harry Vardon teeing off. Before motor drives, these were compositional exercises of supreme difficulty: Beldam had to have the action demonstrated as many times as it took to obtain adequate illustration of each stage. Not until the 1920s would he enjoy equipment equal to capturing all the phases of a single

Advantage Australia: Norman Brookes by Beldam.

action, when he applied a 250-frame-a-second Ultra Rapid Camera to the swings of half a dozen eminent golfers.* This was a way to which Trumper had pointed twenty years earlier.

Finally, consider the backdrop – because, first of all, it *is* a backdrop. Left behind are those classic representations of big cricket, from 'A Cricket Match between the Counties of Sussex and Kent, at Brighton' (1849) to 'An Imaginary Cricket Match: England v Australia' (1887), with their foregrounded crowds and recessed on-field activities. Beldam made the player into the centre of the action, extending a thousandth of a second for all time; the crowd was a blur, like a pictorialist print, or even one of Monet's recent canvases of the Houses of Parliament. Into cricket stepped the cricketer in the role of star, unselfconsciously showcasing the skills that made him so.

Superficially, the crowd, even indistinct, introduces a disjunction to 'Jumping Out', in the sense that it implies a game in progress, at the same time as the deserted outfield suggests otherwise – the result of it being taken, as described, during an intermission in a match. This was, of course, never Beldam's intention. He had as little interest in crowds as those previous artists had shown much. Congregations of spectators feature only occasionally, and incidentally, in his work. Most of his backgrounds are deserted – empty grounds, bare nets – with no attempt made to disguise the nature of

---

* With the Photochrom Company, Beldam published ten two-shilling pamphlets in the series, *The World's Champion Golfers: Their Art Disclosed by the Ultra-Rapid Camera* (1924): they feature strokes from Walter Hagen, Gene Sarazen, Arthur Havers, Abe Mitchell, Roger Wethered and Joyce Wethered, divided into photo sequences of thirty-six displayed in a fold-out section. The Ultra Rapid Camera had been developed by Cinechrome Instruments Company for the British Admiralty to study aircraft-carrier accidents, and it proved a prohibitively expensive venture, each second of film costing thirty shillings. But Beldam persisted, explaining his determination in the same terms as he had with his earlier books: 'The Ultra-Rapid Camera pictures give actual facts – not what the player thinks he does, but what he really does.'

the exercises. Yet as 'Jumping Out' was detached from its context as a plate in an instructional book of other similar plates, and became 'Beldam's Trumper', and finally just 'Trumper', confusion would arise. Was it an artefact of an actual game or was it not? Judges as august as Jack Fingleton and Richie Benaud were perplexed.

Fingleton was long transfixed by plates XXVII and XXVIII. 'Cold figures on paper are drab things when considered in the light of immortality that these two photographs throw upon the cricket world,' he wrote in *Cricket Crisis* (1946). 'Such photographs should be framed and hung in every pavilion in the world for players to see and pay homage to, and seek inspiration from, as they take the field. A coach is incomplete without them.' His faith was shaken, however, by a conversation he recounted in the manuscript for *The Immortal Victor Trumper* (1978):

> That astute man Richie Benaud first of all drew my attention to
> the master picture of all, Trumper jumping down the pitch to drive.
> It is a much-used photograph, but Benaud suggested to me that the
> picture was a fake because it pretended to be of Trumper in a match
> and it was nothing of the sort. The photographer had certainly
> taken the picture of Trumper batting but it was on a practice
> ground and superimposed on the background of a crowd on an
> English ground. It looks like a crowd at Bramall Lane Sheffield,
> with a scoreboard. There is no other person in the picture, no
> fieldsman, no square-leg umpire, no one I accept Benaud's opinion
> that it is a fake, though it greatly disappointed me because I had
> once written that the picture is so inspiring it should be hung in
> all the cricket dressing rooms of the world but no matter.*

---

* In the published version of the book, the third and fourth sentences of this rather obtuse passage were deleted, apparently on the advice of the historian David Frith, but the rest remains.

Both Fingleton and Benaud were misled, effectively, by pictorial cliché. By the time they were scrutinising 'Jumping Out', the huge, receptive, anonymous crowd had become ingrained in the depiction of big-time sport. They took its presence as indicating a match in progress . . . which then, of course, could *not* have been in progress, because of the absence of other figures.

Yet in 1905 this pictorial cliché had yet to emerge. It would be another three years before a significant sporting event was photographed effectually, and then only because at the Games of the IV Olympiad in White City Stadium it was possible to draw close to the athletes, including to the Italian Dorando Pietri as he was overenthusiastically assisted to a controversial marathon victory, overturned on protest. In the most famous image, disoriented Pietri crosses the line with a sturdy, moustachioed official at each elbow; the drama is further magnified by the background, thick with onlookers at what was then the world's largest arena. 'The crowd' as sporting scenery, also providing its imagined soundtrack of approving roar, today passes virtually unremarked; it is an absence of spectators that is likelier to occasion comment. In 'Jumping Out', the background effectively modernises the picture by foretelling the place of fans in future depictions of sport, the massed faces surrounded by murky visual clutter lending a disarmingly contemporary feel.

Does it matter that 'Jumping Out' was to a degree contrived? Arguably less than Fingleton and Benaud supposed. After all, photographs are by nature dissimulations. Time does not stand still. Instants are constantly superseded. Photographs lop life off at the edge of the frame, and yank a fraction of a second out of swiftly forgotten circumstances. Consider what some would regard as the finest sporting photograph of all, Muhammad Ali looming over supine Sonny Liston at Lewiston, Maine in 1965, as seen by Neil

Leifer. The clash looks titanic; in fact, the fight was a seven-round squib. The crowd looks immense: actually, it was the smallest to witness a heavyweight title fight in modern history. Ali seems to have landed a killer blow; rather, he had administered a featherlight touch that nobody saw connect. The victor is not braying defiance; he is admonishing a rival whom he thinks has taken a dive. But, to quote Leifer, none of this mattered: 'This photo became the way people wanted to see Ali, charismatic, tough, confident. The circumstances didn't end up mattering.' It supports the argument of documentary maker Errol Morris that photography reverses the old nostrum: 'It is often said that seeing is believing. But we do not form our beliefs on the basis of what we see; rather, what we see is often determined by our beliefs. Believing is seeing, not the other way round.'

The most important element of 'Jumping Out' is just this: the photograph is the perfect match for the legend, the complete corroboration of the claims, even an anticipation of words attributed to the subject. 'Spoil a bowler's length, and you've got him,' Noble would later quote Trumper as saying – it was 'one of his maxims'. Here he is seen doing just that, invading a space that a thousandth of a second earlier had been effectively conceded, demonstrating that length is not something the bowler sets alone, providing the batsman is quick enough. The picture takes on a hybrid identity as an action photograph that effectively serves as a portrait, in fulfilment of the idea that athletes are defined by their deeds.

All the foregoing facets lay encoded when 'Jumping Out' was published in *Great Batsmen*: the implied commentaries, the subversive blur, the invitations to consider the image as part of a continuous action in front of a reverential crowd, and to relate it to previously held convictions about the aesthetic superiority of Trumper's batting. In the near-term, it also evinced sport's unpredictability. The

*The Governor of the Colony (Sir Henry Barkly) was present in his Box on the Stand and the Game was stayed in situ for the photograph, — but the Sitting Bath not in an amiable mood just then !!!*  B.J.

*Cricket Match at Melbourne, Australia. 1860.*
*Between New South Wales & Victoria (Hot wind blowing.)*

THE TYRANNY OF DISTANCE: Action and proximity were beyond Barrett Johnstone when he took Australia's oldest surviving cricket photograph at the MCG in 1860 (top); artworks like 1887's 'The Imaginary Cricket Match' by Robert Ponsonby Staples and George Barrable (bottom) were better able to capture an instant, while still falling short of intimacy.

1899 AND ALL THAT: In the earliest film footage of Australian cricketers, at Cheltenham (top right), the newsreel cameraman somehow captures Victor Trumper in characteristic attitude (top left). The twenty-one-year-old's first tour of England was also a pilgrimage to places weighted with imperial meaning, like Nelson's flagship HMS *Victory* (bottom).

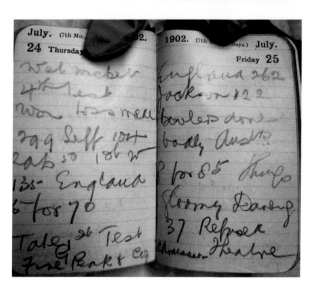

MAKING HIS MARK: In repose on his first tour, Victor Trumper stopped to carve his initials into a dressing-room balcony at Lord's (top); and to receive the tribute of a bat from the past master W. G. Grace (middle). Three years later, he kept a diary, briskly noting the first century before lunch on a Test's opening day: 'Self 104' (bottom).

FOCUS ON TRUMPER: Bewitched by the Trumper of 1902, amateur cricketer
and photographer George Beldam snapped him from afar during the Test at
The Oval (top) and in the nets at Lord's soon after (bottom). With three further
years' experience, Beldam would immortalise his subject at the same locations.

THE BATSMAN OF THE YEAR

*K. S. Ranjitsinhji jumping out to drive. An action-photograph taken by G. W. Beldam at the County Ground, Hove, on the last day of the Sussex Cricket Season, 1904.*

PIN-UP BOY: Prince Ranjitsinhji, most exotic of Edwardian cricketers, flashed before readers of *C. B. Fry's Magazine* in 1904 as an example of Beldam's art. 'The picture, more or less, speaks for itself,' wrote an appreciative Fry – a rare concession.

OVAL-SHAPED: In 1902, local hero Bobby Abel demonstrates 'running out to drive' on his home ground The Oval, static and earthbound (top); the background which George Beldam would reduce to a suggestive blur can also be seen in a 1906 view of the ground and its precincts (bottom), including the Clayton Arms loudly spruiking *Sporting Life*.

VICTOR TRUMPER                                                    PLATE XXVII

Jumping out for a straight drive. Shoulders, arms, and wrists will all come into the stroke.

VICTOR TRUMPER                                                    PLATE XXVIII

Finish of a stroke exactly the same as in Plate XXVII. These two pictures together show
Victor Trumper's drive to perfection.

STROKE OF GENIUS: Stages in the Trumper straight drive shown 'to perfection'
across a double page in 1905's *Great Batsmen* by Beldam and Fry.

## THE SPORTSMAN'S LIBRARY.

*(Our illustrations are reproduced from "Great Batsmen: Their Methods at a Glance," by George W. Beldam and Charles B. Fry, by permission of the publishers, Messrs. Macmillan and Co., Ltd.)*

There is a delightful simplicity in the text, which is Mr. C. B. Fry's contribution. The writer clearly and forcibly explains each photograph in as few words as possible. His first subject is, of course, Dr. Grace, to whom the book is dedicated, and than whom, apart from his position in the cricket world, no finer model could have been selected. Next follow K. S. Ranjitsinhji, Victor Trumper, C. B. Fry, Clem Hill, F. S. Jackson, R. A. Duff, A. C. MacLaren, M. A. Noble, Tom Hayward, R. E. Foster, J. T. Tyldesley, George Hirst, L. C. H. Palairet, J. H. Sinclair, W. W. Armstrong, G. L. Jessop, and W. G. Quaife. Part II. of the book is entitled, "Strokes Illustrated," and the plates here include photographs of many more notable batsmen.

K. S. RANJITSINHJI.

*"This is the famous so-called leg glance, which is perhaps the best known and most admired of Ranjitsinhji's strokes."*

G. L. JESSOP.

*"At first sight the batsman here appears to be beginning an ordinary forward stroke to a ball outside the off-stump. . . . But in point of fact we see here the beginning of a stroke which hits the ball to square leg from well outside the off-stump."*

"THE LOSS OF THE MALPASIA." By J. St. A. Jewell. (Yachtsman Publishing Co.) A collection of real sea stories, told by one who has evidently served under the red ensign, and very well told, too, for the author has a fund of humour in him which mingles pleasantly with the flavour of the salt sea-spray which pervades most of the yarns. The first tale tells of the wreck of a mail-boat, which was run on to a rock, while the fourth officer, who should have been on the bridge in charge, was making love to a lady passenger elsewhere. "The Line of Burling's Drift" is one of the funny stories. It concerns the adventures of an old tub of a vessel which was anchored well to windward of a fleet of smart cutters, yawls, and motor-boats, in order to sail the first thing in the morning. In the middle of the night, however, a gale unexpectedly sprang up, and the old craft started drifting, smashing up all more delicate and expensive boats one by one until she fetched up alongside Southend Pier.

"ARCHERS OF THE LONGBOW." By Arthur Moore. (Constable, 6s.) This is properly described as an "exorbitant" story, for a wilder plot never entered the head of modern writer, nor was more cleverly worked out into such a comedy of errors. A young fellow fresh from college is fascinated by a pretty girl, who, he discovers, resides with a Mr. Plimsol Drew, who carries on the business of "expert adviser." Consulting with a 'Varsity chum, they resolve to invent a case which will require expert advice, and so possibly obtain an introduction to the fair unknown. Accordingly an Anarchist plot with conspirators, an injured Olga and bomb, all complete, is promptly organised, and related to the adviser with such circumstantial detail that he is completely deceived. Not so the young lady, however, and she invents counterplots, and they get most horribly mixed up, but it is too good a story to spoil by entering into further particulars. It will pay for reading.

"PARK LANE." By Percy White. New edition. (Constable, 2s. 6d. net.) The fact that it has reached another edition speaks more loudly in a book's favour than a hundred reviewers; but this is really a very charming novel, including a prettily told love story, and flavoured with delicate satire and up-to-date cynicism. It is relieved by an old bachelor of sixty odd, who has been the *deus ex machina* to bring about the marriage between two young people who, however well they may have been fitted for each other by nature, were certainly opposed by birth and position, as their parents were the most bitter enemies. The girls father was a vulgar, assertive man, a company promoter and financier, while the young man's parent was a member of the aristocracy who had been used by the other as a call bird, so that it may be imagined that there was no love lost between the families. However, all comes right in the end.

"RHYMES OF THE EAST AND RE-COLLECTED VERSES." By Dum Dum. (Constable; 5s. 6d. net.) The majority of these verses have appeared at various times in the pages of *Punch*, but were well worth rescuing from that literary "blend" and given a chance to flourish on their own merits, which they certainly should do, for some of them are particularly clever, and most of them full of humour.

"STORIES AND ESSAYS." By Kate Scanlen. (Henry Drane; 3s. 6d.) This is an unfortunate mixture of fiction and fact, for the subjects do not amalgamate very well. "Pickles" is a pathetic little anecdote of a small boy's first love, which occurs on the voyage home from the Cape, but it is not of sufficient importance to take the leading place in a book of this sort. By the way, where was the corrector to the press when "Medical Men and their Bedside Manners" was being put into type!

THE suggestion that a man learnt his game from a book is generally regarded as a reference of contempt. The inference was justified before the art of illustration had reached its present stage of perfection, and authors candidly admitted that oral instruction and instruction by example were absolutely necessary. But the enormous strides which have been made, during recent years, in rapid photography have almost worked a revolution. In such a volume as that issued by Messrs. Macmillan and bearing the above title, we have not a few plates to illustrate the meanings conveyed in the letterpress, but deductions drawn from no fewer than 600 photographs. A run through the pictures will surprise the reader. He will see

VICTOR TRUMPER.

*"The finish of a cut. The bat has been completely turned over by the wrists."*

famous cricketers in positions in which he can never have remembered seeing them on the field, and positions which will seem to him to be exaggerated. But close inspection will reveal to him a certain grace in all the movements portrayed. Mr. G. W. Beldam's camera shows us that G. L. Jessop has even less respect for style than most of us had imagined, whilst, for his photographs, R. E. Foster might almost have posed, so well does he conform to orthodox methods.

F. S. JACKSON.

*Captain of England XI., 1905.*

---

THE MORTAL VICTOR TRUMPER: A newsreel camera records Trumper's 1915 funeral procession to Waverley Cemetery (top); Victorian cricketers paid their respects after the war in a very different Australia (bottom).

MR. J. C. DAVIS.

THE LEGEND LIVES ON: J. C. Davis, Frank Iredale, Sir Neville Cardus and Jack Fingleton (clockwise from top left) kept fresh the Trumper story in print. 'To change the old saying about the strawberry,' Cardus wrote in 1929, 'God no doubt could create a better batsman than Victor Trumper had He wished but so far He hasn't.'

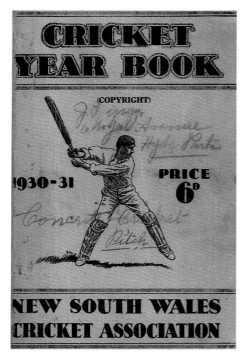

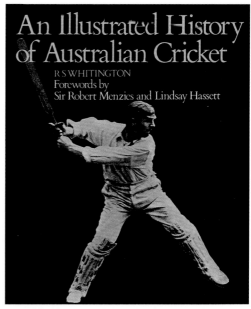

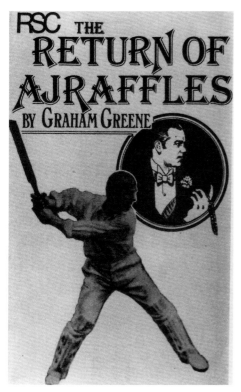

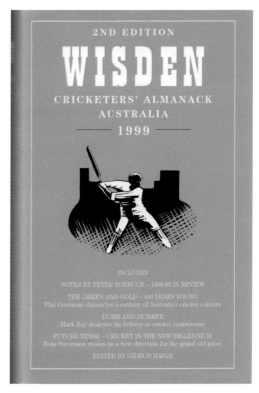

COVER POINT: As Bradman rewrote the statistics therein, the NSW Cricket Association put Trumper on the cover of its yearbook (top left), where he remained for twenty-five years. Perhaps no image has adorned so many cricket book covers since.

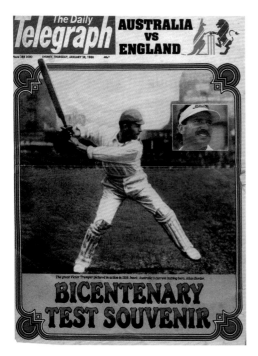

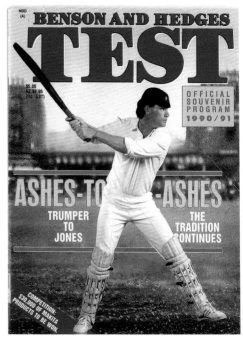

WE CAN DO IT: Trumper goes colour for the Bicentenary Test (top left), likewise his emulators Dean Jones (top right) and Belinda Clark (bottom). Photographer Ian Kenins even posed Clark on Trumper's native heath, Moore Park.

TRUMPER THE SALESMAN: The icon sells a beer (top) and a band (left).

TRUMPER IN INDIA: In *Sport & Pastime* in 1952 (middle); by artist Balaji Venugopal in 2014 (bottom right).

THE ART OF CRICKET: Beldam's Trumper reinterpreted by (clockwise from top left) Judith Dobie, Peter Young, Russell Ayres, Dave Thomas and John Spooner.

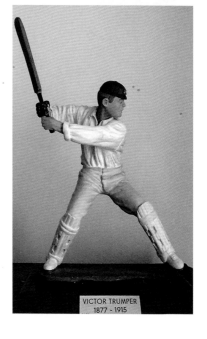

THE CRAFT OF CRICKET: Beldam's Trumper (clockwise from top left) in china, in chalk, in silver, in resin and in tapestry.

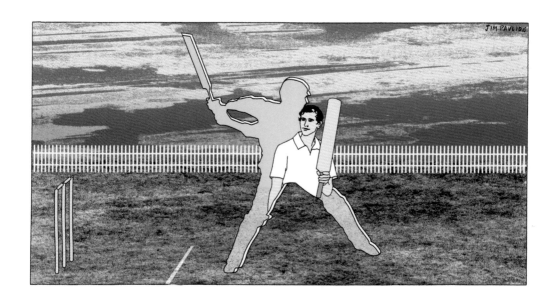

THE SPIRIT OF CRICKET: Beldam's Trumper revived by *The Age*'s Jim Pavlidis to celebrate Ashton Agar in 2013 (top); evoked by the *Daily Telegraph*'s John Tiedemann to mourn Philip Hughes in 2014 (bottom).

day Beldam studied him at The Oval, Trumper was at the peak of his fame; by the time it was available for public consumption, he was coming off the poorest series of his career.

•

'An ordinary batsman who makes nearly 1400 runs before the middle of August is usually heartily patted on the back,' reported *Cricket* as the Tests of 1905 ended. 'But Trumper is not an ordinary batsman.' And of those first-class runs only a meagre 125 in seven completed innings had come against England, preluding a succession of bold but brittle Australian batting performances in a 2–0 defeat. 'There is too much attack about our batting,' complained Leslie Poidevin in *The Referee*. 'It is all very fine for the spectators, but one is not so sure that it is very fine for the team.'

Such criticism reversed that of just a few years earlier. Australian batting had then been too stodgy; now it was too stimulating. It marred the transformation for which the Australians had recently been commended. At the outset of the 1905 tour, *The Field* acclaimed Trumper and his teammates for having 'thrown off the stiffness which characterised the play of some of their precursors' with a 'very exceptional amount of daring', blessed by 'the "eye" which enables Ranji to execute his marvellous *tours de force*'. By the end, *The Field* was tut-tutting in similar terms: 'It may be doubted whether the plan of making a *tour de force* of every stroke and trusting almost entirely to the "eye", of which Trumper is so brilliant an exponent, can be recommended for long wear.'

It's this, perhaps, that has led to the regular misdating of 'Jumping Out' as being from '1902' – the desire to link the photograph to that great pageant of success rather than its muted follow-up. Though

Victor Trumper perhaps *should* have been immortalised in 1902, Beldam was not equipped to do so. There exists a gulf in proficiency between the photographs Beldam was obtaining while Trumper set new batting standards and while he was subtly disappointing them three years later. 'Jumping Out' captures Trumper not at the peak of his powers, but during a diminuendo in his form as his scores and perhaps also his health wavered. He is a man with a decade to live. The photograph might even be thought a hint of this in its resemblance to the genre of the photo finish, automatically generated in horseracing and athletics: Trumper is racing against mortality's encroachments, time's ravages, memory's fading.

The opposite is true of the only surviving newsreel footage of Trumper in a match – also the oldest of a Test in Australia. In December 1910, a *Pathé Animated Gazette* cameraman was present for the opening day of the Sydney Test between Australia and South Africa. He got one glimpse of Trumper – being run out by a direct hit from point on the impetuous call of his opening partner, Warren Bardsley. Trumper was just beginning an extraordinary late-career efflorescence: this thwarted cameo of 27 from thirty-eight balls commenced a ten-innings sequence of 774 runs at 96.75. Yet against Beldam's frozen thousandth of a second, this fifteen seconds of motion has never stood any chance of being remembered. Who cares about a batsman sprawling, picking himself up and walking off, even if he is about to compile a great quantity of runs? In the dawning competition between image and achievement, then, image opened up an early lead – an inference of the fame of 'Jumping Out' is that an image memorable enough will tend over time to draw achievement towards it.

Although not quite yet. For there is a concluding irony to the creation of cricket's first great image. Beldam's photograph was cordially received but not rapturously. The gravure did not sell out; nor did the others. Despite the critical acclaim they enjoyed, *Great Batsmen* and its sequel were too expensively priced to sell in great quantities. We are accustomed now to the idea of content 'going viral', electrifying the world in an instant. A hundred years ago there was neither the telecommunications nor the reprographic technology for this to happen. Wire transmission of images was still a dream; even in illustrated weeklies, such as *Illustrated Sporting and Dramatic News* in England and *The Australasian*, the quality of halftone reproduction was indifferent. The legend of the inaugural cricketer of the visual age would be established in other ways before returning to the image for, as it were, verification.

# 7

# 'I FELL IN LOVE WITH HIM AT ONCE'

'You want me to talk about Victor Trumper? Well, I warn you that if I start
you won't be able to stop me and that it will be with tears in my eyes.'
– ALBERT VINCENT, player with Redfern CC and captain of North Sydney
CC 1909–33, quoted in *Captains Outrageous?*, R. S. Whitington (1971)

At 2.15 p.m. on 31 January 1903, Victor Trumper took his partner Dan
Gee with him to open the batting for Paddington against Redfern.
It was the first time he had been seen in grade cricket since returning
from his triumphs in England, and the crowd at Redfern Oval was
swelling. Shortly the onlookers would be ducking for cover. Fifty
was on the board in twenty minutes, Gee's share of it 5. The hundred
was raised in forty-five minutes, 200 in seventy-five minutes, 300

'Wizard of the Willow': *Town and Country Journal*, 29 January 1913.

With the outbreak of war, Trumper appeared briefly in a couple of patriotic causes, but dropped from view as his illness worsened, retiring to his home, then to St Vincent's Hospital. Various stories circulated of his declining months. In a 1930 biography of Rev. Raymond Preston, Trumper was quoted as telling the Methodist evangelist that he had offered himself to Christ: 'I began to pray and asked God to save me, and He did, and I know it's all right, and if the worst comes, I shall go to the better place, where there is no suffering, and I shall be there when you come, to welcome you.' Making peace was the theme of another story narrated later by Bert Shortland concerning their Gordon clubmate Iredale, who had by then succeeded Bowden as NSWCA secretary:

> When Victor was practically dying I saw him and told him Frank had given a message for him, and Vic said: 'Tell Frank I am having my final knock out. The Greatest Umpire of all will shortly give his decision, and *I know it will be "Out"*, but I have always tried to play the game, and I am not afraid. Tell Frank to let bygones be bygones.' When Frank received this message, he was overcome, and said: 'Victor is the finest sport of all.'

Doubtless this was the sentiment at Waverley Cemetery on that June day of milky sunshine. Members of the NSWCA mourned alongside players they had suspended in 1906, members of the board alongside players they had essentially exiled in 1912; representatives of the NSW Rugby League stood graveside with representatives of the NSW Rugby Union, having been irreconcilable since the split in their game. A wreath from the Melbourne CC reposed among floral tributes from those who had sought its annihilation; it received less attention than a wreath in the colours of the German flag, which turned out to be from the Somerset County Cricket Club. Confusion about Trumper's origins remained unexamined to the end: he was reported as variously thirty-six, thirty-seven and thirty-eight.

It was the epilogue to an era that the participants were unaware had already ended: with a winding-down of the game's administration, first-class cricket would not resume the following summer. Two years later, a bigger and angrier Sydney funeral, that of the boxer Les Darcy, would involve an instant addition to Australian martyrology. The development of the Trumper legend would be a slower-forming affair, partly influenced by sentiments Davis cited in his reporting of the funeral. For this he pulled down his copy of Beldam's *Great Batsmen* and reproduced Fry's verdict: 'Victor Trumper is, perhaps, the most difficult batsman in the world to reduce to words.'

# 9

# 'SEE HIM AND MARVEL!'

'Gather round me, you fellows of the younger cricketing generation,
and I'll try and give you a pen-picture of the Immortal of the Bat – Victor
Trumper. I saw kings of the willow before him, and I have seen all the
giants since the Grim Reaper said, "Out," to the Peerless One, but no
batsman before or after him, in my generation, so truly revealed the
soul of cricket to me as did Trumper, the Imperishable.'
– *Northern Star* (Lismore), 5 November 1927

Not everyone at Victor Trumper's funeral was a hardened veteran of
the decade of administrative strife. Among younger mourners was a
gifted twenty-year-old law student, secretary of the cricket club in
whose second XI he played. Herbert Vere Evatt probably accom-
panied University CC elder Tom Garrett. He was destined for a
brilliant career; but first, like his country, he would have to outlast
a bitter war.

Australia was about to receive a gruelling initiation in the grieving of life cut short. Within a couple of years, Evatt would lose both brothers and suffer the desolating sense that had he gone to war he could have saved them. 'Oh! Dear God, I yearn/For those dear boys who never shall return,' he wrote in a self-lacerating sonnet. Eleven University CC players likewise failed to come back; so did two youthful mourners at Trumper's funeral, his state teammates Tibby Cotter and Norman Callaway.

In the course of war, in fact, funerals of the size of Trumper's would slip from fashion. Historians regard World War I, a wave of random violent mass fatality that left the bereaved without bodies to mourn over, as a watershed in rituals of death and modes of consolation. In Australia, one in five of those who left did not return, and every second household experienced loss. Grief grew more intense, more private, less ostentatious. Much tends to be made of attendance at Trumper's funeral, of Australians turning aside from war to honour a great sportsman; more properly the funeral was a last gasp of former customs. [*]

What *was* a match for the times was Trumper's life – bold, vital and cut short after service to greater glory. Leslie Poidevin's obituary in the *Sydney Morning Herald* made the martial connection explicit: 'The hero of many of the most historic battles of the greensward, and withal the most modest of men, having "played the game" all his life, he has at last bravely answered the final call all too soon.' Trumper's death would be noted in *Wisden* in the distinguished company of

---

[*] Typical in this respect, Jack Pollard's *The Turbulent Years of Australian Cricket* (1987) ('Despite the importance of the war news, Trumper's death, at the age of only 37, was splashed across the front pages of Australia's newspapers') and Peter FitzSimons' *Great Australian Sports Champions* (2006) ('It took a lot for anything other than the news of the war to dominate newspaper billboards at that time – when so many of our own were fighting for their lives on Gallipoli – but the death of Victor Trumper accomplished that easily, and not just in Australia').

W. G. Grace, who perished to a heart attack in October 1915, but was somehow closer in nature to the obituaries in the same edition for the nearly 200 young cricketing men killed on duty. Certainly a young major in the 60th Rifles serving in France thought so. As a schoolboy, H. S. Altham had seen Trumper's maiden Test hundred; as a schoolteacher, he would later write cricket's first significant synoptic history. 'I can remember . . . feeling no real sorrow for W.G. passing Homeric and legendary into Elysian fields,' he recalled, 'but an almost personal pain that Trumper's gallant spirit and matchless grace should have been called so early from the world it enriched.' *Called so early*: it was not a term that Altham, recipient of the Distinguished Service Order and Military Cross, would have used lightly.

Elsewhere in the same lists of what has become its most famously poignant number, *Wisden* reported the death of Sub-Lieutenant Rupert Brooke, who left a corner of an Aegean field forever England by succumbing to sunstroke on Lemnos in April 1915. The almanack scrupulously documented his 1906 Rugby School season of nineteen wickets at 14 before noting his having 'gained considerable reputation as a poet'. It was a time, in fact, when poetry often seemed the only adequate form of expression and source of solace – not necessarily the poetry being written, deepeningly bleak, but the stocks of verse already dedicated to premature death, such as Milton's 'Lycidas', Tennyson's 'In Memoriam', Shelley's 'Adonaïs', Kipling's 'Recessional', Housman's 'A Shropshire Lad'. C. J. Dennis grumbled about all this high-falutin' stuff when he farewelled his protagonist at Gallipoli in *The Moods of Ginger Mick* (1916): ''E found a game 'e knoo, an' played it well;/An' now 'e's gone. Wot more is there to tell?' But the space of special honour that sport reserved for its dead took particular comfort in Housman's *fin-de-siècle* words:

Now in Maytime to the wicket
Out I march with bat and pad:
See the son of grief at cricket
Trying to be glad . . .
Smart lad, to slip betimes away
From field where glory does not stay
And early though the laurel grows
It withers quicker than the rose.
Eyes the shady night has shut
Cannot see the record cut,
And silence sounds no worse than cheers
After earth has stopped the ears:
Now you will not swell the rout
Of lads that wore their honours out,
Runners whom renown outran
And the name died before the man.

This eventuality would now not befall Trumper. In a sense, all athletes die twice, the first time with the end of their competitive span. For Trumper the twilight was brief and the darkness descended swiftly. The tragedy that befell his family when he left a widow with a nine-year-old daughter and an eighteen-month-old son also relieved his image of the toll of decline. 'I have one great satisfaction regarding Victor Trumper,' wrote Charlie Macartney, a Gordon teammate and protégé. 'I never saw him grow old as a cricketer.' As J. C. Davis concluded in his eulogy in *The Referee*: 'Those whom the gods love die young.'

•

A corollary of this is that gods can seem ambivalent about those to whom they grant longer life. This is also evident in the Trumper story. As war wound on, the sun set on a whole sporting world. The leisure society of which C. B. Fry and George Beldam had been gifted members would reconvene afterwards in reduced circumstances and darker hues.

Fry's gilded youth and exhilarating maturity, noted his contemporary Lord Birkenhead, petered out 'into a somewhat desultory and disappointed career'. He dabbled in diplomacy, advising Ranji at the League of Nations. He detoured into politics, thrice running unsuccessfully as a Liberal. He fantasised of a movie career, making several trips to Hollywood. Most of the time he wandered the TS *Mercury* in a uniform that purportedly made him 'look every inch like six admirals', while remaining a clear subordinate to his mirthless and tyrannical wife, whose boy cadets endured a regime heavy on deprivation, sadism and surveillance – they answered to numbers rather than their names, had their bowel movements documented and their genitalia examined daily. Thanks to Charles Hoare's will, Fry enjoyed a twenty-five-room mansion on spacious grounds with a butler, servants and a Rolls-Royce – but not much else. In the late 1920s he suffered an acute mental breakdown.

Six years' convalescence later, Fry found a niche with an idiosyncratic column in the *Evening Standard*, 'C. B. Fry Says' – even if what Fry said, like his flirtation with fascism, did not always show him in a flattering light. Beatie's death in 1946 seemed to cheer him. His biographer Denzil Batchelor recalled Fry's eccentric greeting at her memorial service. 'Look!' Fry exclaimed. 'I'll show you an infallible way to play a googly.' When the chapel bell rang while he was demonstrating, he said: 'Never mind, we'll finish afterwards . . .' But at seventy-four it was too late to act on any of his periodic enthusiasms. On one occasion, Fry professed boredom with cricket and said he would go into racing. 'What as?' Batchelor asked. 'Trainer – jockey – or horse?' So in declining years, Fry would lie awake on the *Mercury* reciting aloud the details of cricket matches he had played. It was not the end anyone had foretold for this most omnicompetent Englishman.

Multiple enthusiasms stretched Beldam thin, too. Having provided the illustrations for no fewer than eight sizeable sporting books within three years, including a pioneering textbook on jujutsu, he also suffered a breakdown, ascribed to overwork. Forty in May 1908, he forsook flannels at Lord's for Savile Row suits in the City, although he maintained his old contacts: he diversified Beldam Packing & Rubber into sporting goods, including partnering J. H. Taylor in the marketing of a 'JH' golf ball, and formed the G. W. Beldam Tyre Syndicate, whose shareholders included his brother Cyril, Ranji and Archie MacLaren. Beldam Packing insulated the boilers of the *Titanic*; four Beldam anti-skid tyres were beneath Lawrence of Arabia's Rolls-Royce during his desert campaigns.

Back to business: Beldam insulates the *Titanic*.

After World War I, George Beldam's life look a racier turn. First he abandoned his wife Gertrude for Margaret Frew Underwood, an old schoolfriend of his daughter, whom he married in June 1921. She bore him a son and a daughter, but their relations were volatile, and they parted. Then he fell in love with his children's twenty-year-old nurse, Christina Thompson, and eloped with her to Biarritz. After a while they took up residence in a village in Surrey where Beldam lived under an assumed name, and Christina bore a daughter. Margaret, however, would not consent to a divorce until just before Christina gave birth to twins, a boy and girl, in June 1930.

The couple finally settled on 24 acres (8 hectares) near an old market town, Farnham, where Beldam took pleasure in growing rhododendrons and driving a twelve-cylinder Packard with fold-out seats for his third family. A certain bohemianism may even have been in the blood. In November 1937, brother Cyril was involved in a scandalous breach-of-promise case that became a tabloid sensation: the inamorata was an artist's model with two sisters. 'I am not going to put Mr Beldam before you as a man of morals,' admitted his defence counsel, former attorney-general Sir Patrick Hastings. 'He has behaved extraordinarily badly. But this is not a court of morals. These three sisters have put their heads together to rob Mr Beldam.' No sooner had the court agreed than George suffered a fatal coronary, leaving his young widow with three children – again, not perhaps the end one would have prophesied for this cultured and eclectic English gent.

On the other side of the world, Sydney's *Referee* recalled Beldam's legacy of *Great Batsmen* and *Great Bowlers and Fielders*: 'These books hand down to two generations in picture and prose the beauties and the methods of masters who have passed on. These include several Australians. The man closes his chapter. The book never.' With that, at least, Beldam might have rested content.

•

Of sport as well as of society, postwar rebuilding would never be quite complete. By the time cricket resumed, only Warwick Armstrong and Hanson Carter remained of the recalcitrant six, and briefly. Administrators found their younger players, many of them having served, more tractable, happy enough to be playing at all – some had undergone acute hardships, such as all-rounder Charles Kelleway, four times wounded, and keeper Bert Oldfield, five months in hospital with shell shock after being blown up at Polygon Wood. In England's hobbled economy, cricket made faltering progress. Amateurism was a social luxury hard to afford. In the 1920s the proportion of amateurs in county cricket halved, and their quality was thinner. England's foremost cricket hero, Jack Hobbs, hardly resembled Jovian Grace, versatile Fry or vivid Ranji: a professional, the son of a Cambridge groundsman, he personified in his batting and bearing the scaled-down ambitions of English suburbia – dedicated, unassuming, thrifty, abstemious, a proud tradesman who nonetheless deferred to amateur inferiors. And although the distinction between gentlemen and players would survive another world war, England's foremost cricket personalities through that time would file chiefly through the professional gate: Woolley, Hammond, Hendren, Sutcliffe, Larwood, Hutton, Compton.

The scene was also psychically bleaker. Worcestershire's Fred Root, who opened England's bowling ten years after he was told war wounds in France would prevent him playing again, recalled rolls of honour in every county pavilion, and memories everywhere: 'Village shrines, the larger war memorials of the towns and cities, and all things which are built "for ever to acknowledge those great sacrifices" bear names associated with the game of cricket. And we who were spared – *remember –*.' In his travelogue *England Over* (1927), *Times* journalist Dudley Carew watched the Eton v Harrow match with a dignified black-clad woman for whom it was the annual pilgrimage in honour of her lost Harrovian son: 'The things he was going to do! He loved cricket so.' It is a stage without an end: '"There are years to come," she said slowly. "Years and years, years and years."' Carew's other two cricket books, *The Son of Grief* (1936), a cheerless novel of professional cricket, and *To the Wicket* (1946), a set of pensive essays, both nod to Housman in their titles.

In *Cricket in Firelight* (1935), a memoir of *Observer* journalist Richard Binns, pre-war cricket lay preserved as if in amber, the relic of an irrecoverable comfort and innocence. Before joining up, Binns and his 'cheery, happy-go-lucky friend' Jerry Murgatroyd had been busy cricketers and fans who rejoiced in cricket talk: of village matches, of Test and Roses matches, of Grace ('The Champion'), of Ranjitsinhji ('the shining star from the East') and of Trumper ('the greatest batsman of all time . . . a lion whom no bowler and no pitch could tame'). Returning maimed from 'the Last Great Match of All', they spent 'many days of sickness and disability' consoling themselves with their cricket memories until Murgatroyd's death, and the toll on Binns of 'a wartime legacy of broken health'. The book, popular enough to be reprinted twenty years later, is Binns' attempt to recreate their chats: 'In the lowering firelight the enlarging shadows grew more vaguely grotesque and moved more slowly on the walls as Jerry Murgatroyd called back one after another these grey spirits of cricket past, noble shadows that even in the ghostliness of memory still bore themselves as proudly as in the full panoply of hot action on the field.' Trumper, whom the pair saw as boys in 1902, is evoked in all his vitality as 'a young athletic god trailing clouds of glory about him as he moved', then mourned in his premature mortality: 'It is hard to think that such graciousness as Victor Trumper brought to cricket and to life should be foredoomed to travel the dusty way of common mortality and decay. Victor Trumper died in 1915, after a painful illness, in his thirty-eighth year.' The implicit parallel is with the dimming of Jerry's once brilliant light. The question was now how best to remember, in a fashion that did not become its own form of torment.

•

Shortly after World War I ended, a man visiting his brother's grave in Waverley Cemetery was approached by a woman asking directions to Victor Trumper's final resting place. The man, he recalled in a letter to *The Referee*, asked if she was a relative. No, she said, nor even a friend. 'I belong to the country, and when visiting Sydney I have seen him play cricket on several occasions,' she said. 'He struck me as being such a fine sportsman that I have come out this afternoon just to see the place where he is laid to rest.' It wasn't surprising that she was having trouble: the only marking on the tomb was 'VIC' incised in the freestone railing. Crown Street School had opened a fund to erect a memorial, but as of three and a half years after Trumper's death he had no headstone.

Like Australia itself, cricket was in straitened circumstances. The NSWCA had a bank balance of £9 11s. A suspended plan for a memorial drinking fountain in Trumper's honour was revived, and subscriptions invited. 'To many of the present-day players, Vic Trumper is little more than a name,' commented 'Point' in the *Newcastle Sun*. 'I am afraid many of them do not know their cricket history as they should . . . Let the memorial be worthy of him.' But barely had the lists opened than the association learned that Trumper's widow was in financial hardship: it pragmatically gave her the bulk of £229 raised, retaining just enough to pay for a plaque at the rear of the Sheridan Stand.

Trumper's memory remained up for claiming. In January 1919, Victorian cricketers made a pilgrimage to Waverley Cemetery and laid a wreath blessed by Rev. E. H. Sugden, the venerable master of Melbourne's Queen's College. Victor Trumper, said Sugden, had been the personification of amateurism: 'Had the German nation been imbued with the same sporting spirit, the war, involving so much bloodshed, may never have occurred.' The *Sydney Morning Herald* dedicated a lengthy editorial to the Victorians' 'graceful and appropriate' gesture hoping that cricket would revert to being played in 'Trumper's spirit', forgetfully opining that it was 'never so popular or so free from disputes as when both players and officials remembered that it was a game'. Trumper's memory affirmed imperial ties, too. When MCC visited six years later, their well-liked captain Arthur Gilligan enhanced his popularity by laying a wreath at the SCG plaque in honour of 'the greatest batsman the world has ever seen'. Trumper, Gilligan explained to widespread approval, had been his 'one idol on the cricket field', too.

Agreement on a more substantial monument remained elusive. In August 1923, perhaps inspired by the recent example of the Grace Gates installed at Lord's, Paddington Council announced their intention to rename Hampden Oval in honour of the greatest player it had hosted. At the last moment, however, they were unexpectedly thwarted by Lands Minister Walter Wearne, who was unpersuaded of the case for a rededication. Viscount Hampden had been an inoffensive state governor in the 1890s; Trumper's 'success in the cricket field', the minister felt, was 'not sufficient reason why the name should be changed'. Needless to say, Wearne courted considerable disagreement, even in his own ranks. At a public meeting, the speaker of the Legislative Assembly, Daniel Levy, distanced himself from his fellow Nationalist and advertised his support for the campaign. Other speakers joined in. What was an English governor compared to Trumper? How much fame for Australia had been won by 'all the Joe Cooks and high commissioners'? Wearne remained unmoved. Yet there was emerging a way to recapture Trumper without the rigmarole of public collections and ministerial petitionings – and it had been around twenty years.

In an era when the simplest image can be proliferated and distributed so easily, it can be hard to imagine the scarcities and restrictions of the past. *Great Batsmen* had been an expensive book; the few copies of the gravure of 'Jumping Out' that had made it to Australia were in private hands.* One hung inside the door of the NSWCA's premises at George Street, where Leslie Poidevin described it for the *Sunday Times* in November 1922: 'It is a near perfect illustration of the essential features in the correct execution of the off-drive. The swing of the bat, the poise of the body, the positions of the left leg and foot in the air ready to go forward and come down, with the bat to meet the ball – it is a classic photograph, to my view, and I commend its study to *anyone having the opportunity to view it.*' [my italics] Because the quality of halftone illustration on Australian newsprint was insufficient to do the image justice, the reader had to take Poidevin's word for it.

---

* In Ceylon on his way to Australia in 1936, Fry mentioned that he had recently been asked for a copy of *Great Batsmen* by Princess Mary, learned that the book was 'not to be had anywhere', and at last obtained a copy for fifteen guineas. Clem Hill attested both volumes' rarity in a 1940 letter to a correspondent in Surrey: 'The two great books *Batsmen & Bowlers* written by C.B.Fry & pictures taken by Beldam was [sic] wonderful – Don't know whether [you] can get it now – but if procurable get it.'

In England, Beldam's work enjoyed continued cachet: his Trumper photographs featured in the new edition of *The Badminton Book of Cricket* (1920), Pelham Warner's *Book of Cricket* (1920) and Gilbert Jessop's *Cricket and How to Play It* (1925); 'Jumping Out' took pride of place on the office wall at Fleet Street's Cricket Reporting Agency, *Wisden*'s inner sanctum. As it should, thought H. S. Altham in his ongoing 'History of Cricket' series in *Cricketer*: 'To try to reduce to words the art of this consummate batsman is almost an impertinence, but to those who never saw him at his best I would suggest that they should study the glorious series of photographs of Trumper in action contained in Beldam and Fry's *Great Batsmen*. From these they will catch at least a reflection of the ease, the balance, the perfect naturalness that made him surely the most fascinating batsman to watch in the history of the game.' But when Noble published *The Game's the Thing* (1926), with its lengthy and lyrical evocation of Trumper, he omitted 'Jumping Out', as though his friend should linger chiefly in the mind's eye.

Then, in October 1927, the *Sydney Mail* took a chance. The fifty-page Sydney weekly had been redesigned to lead the market in illustration, using a new Hoe Fine Art Rotary Web Press, and printing exclusively on art paper. Its circulation had surged during the war, and its pictorial ambitions grown, not least in cricket. English-born staff photographer Herbert Fishwick persuaded the paper's owners to indulge him with an English-made accessory, a 43-inch (109 cm) Ross & Co. lens, for his Graflex camera. Such lenses had been developed for photography from aeroplanes and balloons, but they also proved a superb means of bridging the distances involved in photographing cricket, of which Fishwick made a speciality, his signature being the use of diagonal angles from vantages backward of point.

It's likely that Fishwick had a hand when the *Mail* dedicated half a page to a reproduction of the NSWCA's copy of 'Jumping Out'. The context of its Australian rediscovery was a tribute, 'The Standard Set by Victor Trumper', by former Crown Street classmate and Gordon clubmate Bert Shortland. The standard Shortland had in mind was less Trumper's batting than his sportsmanship and good nature: 'There are many modest players, but was ever such modesty blended with such capacity for great achievement? He was well named Victor, and his memory shall endure, a standard for cricketers for ever.' The unadorned grave was now of a piece with these qualities: 'At Waverley by the sea – there he rests! No great headstone covers his resting-place; those who seek may find. Just three magic letters mark the spot, and they are "V I C." Nothing more – as in life, so in death – Modesty.' As far as the batting genius was concerned, Shortland could allow the photograph to do the work, with a little help from the complementary caption:

> To look at this picture (kindly lent by the N.S.W. Cricket Association) is to see Victor Trumper as we used to see him from the pavilions. See him and marvel! It does not show his face clearly, but as an action picture it is wonderful. No hesitancy here. He is stepping out to meet the ball. Strength, grace, and balance, combine to reveal joyous and youthful sense of mastery. What was the secret of this joyous freedom? Simply the beautiful character of Victor. All young players should know all that can be told of him, whose other name was Modesty.

Here was a blissful solution to the challenges of remembrance. No need to worry about monuments; no need to strain for the words and phrases that had always felt inadequate; reproducing 'Jumping Out'

# 'SEE HIM AND MARVEL!'

### Victor !

*To look at this picture (kindly lent by the N.S.W. Cricket Association) is to see Victor Trumper as we used to see him from the pavilions. See him and marvel! It does not show his face clearly, but as an action picture it is wonderful. No hesitancy here. He is stepping out to meet the ball. Strength, grace, and balance, combine to reveal joyous and youthful sense of mastery. What was the secret of this joyous freedom? Simply the beautiful character of Victor. All young players should know all that can be told of him, whose other name was Modesty.*

# The Standard Set by Victor Trumper

### By H. S.

*With the cricket season opening we commend to all players these references to the late Victor Trumper. There is more in cricket than skill in batting, bowling, or fielding. Not only for his wonderful batting will Trumper never be forgotten. His name will always be to cricketers a synonym for sportsmanship, and especially for one phase of sportsmanship—Modesty. There are many modest players, but was ever such modesty blended with such capacity for great achievement? He was well named Victor, and his memory shall endure, a standard for cricketers for ever.*

LAST season the standard of umpiring was often discussed, and some of the "white-coats" had their qualifications challenged by disappointed players. Whether the criticisms were justified is doubtful. An umpire may—and occasionally does—give a wrong decision, but the standard here is probably as good as is possible. I am inclined to question, not the umpires, but the good taste of the players when umpires are attacked, and it may be timely to give a few examples of Victor Trumper's attitude in respect of such ethics.

I went to school with Victor, and played with him, off and on, right up to the end. On one occasion at a school match Vic was given out in a match which was an absolute bump ball, and his team mates were very exasperated. Victor's only remark when he came in was: "Never mind; we will do it next time." And sure enough he did, for he scored 206 not out.

Getting a fast ball on the leg side in a match played by Gordon, Vic. tried to glance, and in doing so the ball just touched the buckle of his pad. Someone in the outfield appealed, and the umpire gave him out. I was batting with him, and told him it was a bad decision. Vic. asked me to walk with him to the pavilion, and on the way he gave me a little lesson about doubting the umpire. When walking into the pavilion a barracker asked him if he was out. Vic.'s reply was: "I had a splendid knock" (he scored 128); "it was about time I was out."

ONCE, when playing Glebe, "Yabba," was really a very amusing barracker, exasperated me, and I suggested to Vic. that the noisy one might be spoken to by the groundsman. Vic.'s reply was: "What! He is one of the Glebe team, and is the best member in it." He would not hear of "Yabba" being stopped.

He regarded "Yabba" as a "character," and took his comments in the right spirit.

Another time when playing in a minor match I appealed for l.b.w., and the batsman was given out by the umpire. Our opponents were patients in a mental hospital. Vic. strolled up to me and quietly said that it was up to us to give the poor fellows as much pleasure as possible, and not to appeal to the umpires—who, by the way, were also patients. You could go on repeating these incidents of Vic.'s sportsmanship. Playing Balmain one day Vic. scored two centuries. I have never seen these quoted when reference is made to double centuries. I happened to be batting with him each time when he reached his 100, and in both knocks he purposely gave his wicket to "Mazie" Sullivan, as he reckoned that he had worked the hardest and he always had a kindly feeling for him.

Finally, Vic. and Frank Iredale were at loggerheads over the Board of Control trouble. When Victor was practically dying I saw him and told him Frank had given me a message for him, and Vic. said: "Tell Frank I am having my final knock out. The Greatest Umpire of all will shortly give his decision, and I know it will be 'Out,' but I have always tried to play the game, and I am not afraid. Tell Frank to let bygones be bygones." When Frank received this message he was overcome, and said: "Victor is the finest sport of all." Poor old Frank has since joined him.

ONE more incident before closing to show the kindly spirit of this greatest of all players. Gordon won the premiership in 1911, and after a keen struggle it came to the final match, Gordon v Redfern. I happened to be a co-selector with Victor for the year. On the Thursday before the match I received a ring from him to go down to his sports shop, and on comparing our teams we differed by one player.

He had included Don Campbell, father of the present interstate cricketer. Now, Don was really not in the first grade in those days. The standard was high. He had, however, been a wonderful worker for the game all his life, and he had the ambition to play in a first-grade match before retiring. Victor knew this, and gratified his desire. The match caused a great deal of interest at the time in Sydney, and 15,000 people went out to Redfern each day. After a keen struggle, although Redfern had to make only 173 runs to win, the bowling proved too deadly and they failed by 37 runs. Victor always tried to give pleasure to others. He was far from well, but at 5 o'clock the Redfern barrackers would not leave the ground until he batted. I tried to persuade him not to go in, but he replied: "I like to please the crowd," and he went in dressed in his ordinary clothes, except that he wore his cricketing boots. He had a great slog, scoring 78 in 34 minutes. This included 10 fours and five "sixers." Arthur Mailey should remember this, as Arthur bowled Victor cheaply in the first innings; but in the second—well! On the Wednesday I received a message from Mr. McGowen, then Premier, to call at his office. When I arrived there Mr. McGowen, Victor, Frank Iredale, and others were present. Vic. then handed me the ball used in the final match. The silver shield on it reads: "From Vic. Trumper to ——, for winning premiership, 1910-11." Here again he showed his great sportsmanship.

CRICKETERS and all sports, you cannot all be champions; but you can all try to emulate his spirit. One quality of sportsmanship is modesty. At Waverley by the sea—there he rests! No great headstone covers his resting-place; those who seek may find. Just three magic letters mark the spot, and they are "V I C." Nothing more—as in life, so in death—Modesty.

*(Continued on Next Page.)*

'The Standard Set by Victor Trumper': vertiginous.

was the equivalent of expressing an artist by his work, or quoting a public man in his own words. It was also to modernise Trumper, to bring him into the pictorial economy of the *Mail*'s well-to-do readership, interested in sport, fashion, travel and a growing Australia. His leap had the optimism of Sydney's stretching across its mighty harbour, the Bridge's progress being one of the *Mail*'s illustrative staples.

Following up Trumper, the *Mail* published another indelible cricket image. Fishwick's subject in November 1928, busily compiling 225 for MCC against New South Wales, was the Englishman Walter Hammond playing a sumptuous cover drive, with keeper Bert Oldfield in seemingly sympathetic attendance, as alert as a gun dog. 'A Vigorous Drive by Hammond' was accorded vigorous

'A Vigorous Drive': Fishwick's Hammond.

treatment, occupying the entirety of the *Mail*'s page five, with a distinguished afterlife ahead.[*] It was at the very least a technical breakthrough. Never able to draw the action toward him, Beldam had had to contrive to meet it halfway; Fishwick's lens now did the work unassisted.

So it was that virtually a quarter of a century after it was taken, 'Jumping Out' began at last to reach a popular audience, and it would become a common sentiment that no Australian cricket location was quite complete without it. It hung in the members stands at the SCG and the MCG. In October 1931, when the government relented and agreed to rechristen Hampden Oval as Trumper Park, Monty Noble unveiled a handsome print in the clubrooms at the tea-break of a charity match. Visitors to the chambers of Bill Dovey, later Gough Whitlam's father-in-law, were impressed by his gravure. Visitors to Bert Oldfield's sports store in Sydney's Hunter Street saw both Beldam's Trumper and Fishwick's Hammond, forming a kind of aesthetic continuum. Hanging on the wall at Crown Street Superior School, 'Jumping Out' was drummed into the next generation. 'You got so used to seeing that picture that after you had been at the school a month you would wake up in the morning and see it in every detail on your bedroom wall,' recalled Colin McCool, then a tiny opening batsman on the fringe of the school XI but destined to play fourteen postwar Tests for Australia. 'Once at Crown Street School, I found my life dominated by the picture and the memory of Trumper. His name was in every conversation, every move we made on the cricket field.'

Personal copies also reappeared. Clem Hill's adorned his cricket reminiscences; Hugh Trumble's was displayed in the window of the

---

[*] Scyld Berry argues for it in *Cricket: The Game of Life* (2015) as 'the most beautifully composed photograph of the most beautiful cricket stroke'.

Orient Line office in Collins Street; Joe Darling's was shown off to federal cabinet when they visited his home in Claremont, Tasmania, in February 1939. Interviewed by journalists, Darling gestured to the photograph as proof of Trumper's superiority to the flat-footed batsmen of the present day: 'He was the boy who would have played the O'Reillys and the Grimmetts. There would have been no fiddling about with him.' 'Jumping Out', then, was taking on a new dimension, as a reference in the conversation of generations. And that conversation was livening up.

•

During his career, several batsmen had been likened in style to Trumper. Similarities had been discerned in his Sydney contemporaries Jim Mackay and Charles Gregory; the appellation of 'the English Trumper' had been settled on both R. E. Foster and Kenneth Hutchings; an elegant batsman from Perth, Ernest Parker, had been anointed 'the West Australian Trumper'. Melancholy fates awaited them all. Mackay's career was ended by a motorcycle accident, aged twenty-seven; Gregory and Foster succumbed to illness, aged thirty-two and thirty-six respectively; Hutchings and Parker were doomed to die on the Western Front.

The mantle was not bestowed indiscriminately, and, in cricket at least, seems to have required a physical resemblance. Charlie Macartney, impudent and irrepressible, was Australia's most exciting batsman after the war. But despite his strong personal kinship with Trumper, stocky Macartney was generally deemed too pugnacious for direct comparison, which he would have disowned anyway. 'I have never seen a batsman to equal Victor Trumper in brilliance,' he insisted. Aesthetes preferred slim, wristy Alan Kippax, an overt

Trumper copyist. As a boy he had followed Trumper to grade games with a scorebook in which he only entered his hero's runs. His mimicry extended to folding his shirtsleeves beyond the elbow, the Trumper way. The name of Trumper was also invoked in other sports, usually when practitioners demonstrated a sense of style or dash. Rugby five-eighth Tom Lawton, jockey Keith Voitre, golfers Joe Kirkwood and George Duncan, tennis players J. O. Anderson, John Bromwich, Daphne Akhurst and Suzanne Lenglen: all were likened to Trumper during the 1920s and 1930s.* *The Bulletin* even described Coil, a much-garlanded turn-of-the-century blue kelpie from Cootamundra, as being 'to the dog world what Victor Trumper was to cricket'.

In the mid-1920s, the Trumper name began rippling through cricket anew, with the appearance of a teenage prodigy. Captain of Balmain District Cricket Club was Arthur Mailey – no longer the dreamy drifter of before the war, but a journalist, cartoonist and raconteur as well as Australia's first-choice leg spinner. It was he who in Sydney's *Sun* alerted the public to his fifteen-year-old clubmate, Archie Jackson, then receiving an initial exposure to senior competition. 'I am not going to compare him with the glorious Victor Trumper at this stage,' wrote Mailey, 'but if wealth of common cricket sense and ability is an asset, then the boy's future is assured.'

Jackson was too young to have seen Trumper. Instead he had imitated Kippax – the tracing of a tracing, as it were. In due course Jackson would work behind the counter of Kippax's Martin Place sports store, too. But rhapsodies for his batting came chiefly from those with memories going back before the war. Not only was

---

\* Duncan also attracted the admiration of George Beldam, who provided the illustrations for his *Present-Day Golf* (1924). In the same year, the golf correspondent of *The Australasian*, 'HC', said that one figure towered above the game: 'That man is George Duncan, the great Aberdonian golfer, and he deserves in all respects to be considered the Victor Trumper of the links. From an Australian gallery's point of view, surely no greater praise than that is possible.'

## LIKE TRUMPER.

ARCHIE JACKSON.
*"How like Victor," said Charlie Trumper, brother of the dead champion, when Jackson was compiling a delightful 183 for Balmain against Gordon on Saturday, "I was just about to say the same thing," replied Arthur Mailey.*

Heir Today: *Daily Standard*, 13 October 1931.

Jackson a pretty bat, but in person shy and modest, a sportsman to his fingertips and a total abstainer to boot – an heir to Trumper in all respects. Doc Evatt, now the Labor member for Balmain, became his unofficial patron. He was praised by Tom Garrett and Charles Bannerman, and became a favourite of J. C. Davis, who was first drawn to Balmain by the advice of a friend: 'He looks to be Victor reborn.' Davis was transfixed.

Jackson was more of a prodigy than Trumper had been. Aged sixteen, he topped the Sydney grade averages; aged seventeen, he made hundreds for New South Wales against Queensland and Tasmania; aged nineteen, he made a ravishing 164 on his Test debut against England at Adelaide Oval. Clem Hill now thought him 'the nearest to Trumper I have seen'. Victor's brother Charlie agreed. Again Mailey counselled against direct comparison, while allowing an indirect one: 'My advice is this – let him work out his shots in his own way, and work out his own methods. You didn't need to tell Victor Trumper how to play bowlers. Cricketers are born not made.' The comparison so exercised readers that Davis found himself asked to adjudicate in *The Referee* in December 1929 as to which of Jackson and Kippax resembled Trumper more profoundly. He peered discriminatingly through his *pince-nez*:

> From the points of view of stance and polished style, Kippax is more like Trumper; and in some of his strokes he is more like Trumper. But in the variety of high-class scoring strokes, in the mastery of placing particularly between the bowler and cover-point, and in the disposition to use high driving on either side of the wicket, the palm goes to Jackson.

Not that Davis was quite ready to countenance a rival to Trumper, whom he praised in familiar terms: 'The master's bat made music to the tunes he loved, not to those his less gifted pals might have loved. It is always so with genius. And a genius Trumper was.' But he concluded broad-mindedly: 'Lucky is the country, lucky the state to have produced a Trumper, a Kippax, a Jackson.' Watching Jackson practise in October 1931, Davis fell into a virtual swoon: 'On Thursday, as one viewed him from a distance making his strokes at the net, it seemed as though Victor Trumper had come back to the old scenes.'

Tragically, Jackson's day was already done: the following month he collapsed in Brisbane, coughing up blood. Now the likeness to Trumper took on a darker complexion: installed in a Blue Mountains sanatorium, Jackson was diagnosed with tuberculosis. At his death in February 1933, he, too, was borne to his resting place by teammates through dense crowds, and his memorial funded by public subscription. Trumper's second coming had been a bittersweet affair. It had also, in a sense, already been overtaken by events.

•

In November 1928, Ben Travers was sitting in the Members Stand at the SCG watching Marylebone play the state side preparatory to the summer's Ashes – the same game, as it happens, in which Herbert Fishwick immortalised Walter Hammond. For the sport-crazy Aldwych farceur, it was the trip of a lifetime – 'a cricket-lover's nirvana'.

Suddenly, Travers recalled, there was a 'striking incident'. As a batsman played a sumptuous cover drive, a local devotee leapt to his feet with a shout of: 'Trumper!' 'He was pulled violently back into his seat and for the moment appeared in danger of being lynched,' the playwright remembered. 'This was near blasphemy.' *This* was twenty-year-old Donald Bradman.

With 87 and 132 not out, Bradman made sure of his Australian selection. In his second Test, like Trumper, he made a century, provoking further comparison, overheard by former Australian prime minister Billy Hughes: 'The experts around me that day compared him with Trumper, some holding he was not in the same class, others strongly contending that he was Trumper's equal.' This series, of course, was simply a prologue to the saga. Within eighteen months Bradman had compiled the highest scores in Test and first-class cricket history on opposite sides of the world, and broken the records for runs in a home summer and runs on an Ashes tour previously held by . . . Victor Trumper. The beamish boy from Bowral was the world's most lauded cricketer. Yet in some circles there were only two cheers. When the NSWCA decided for the first time to place an illustration on the cover of their yearbook in 1930–31, it was not of the man of the moment, but of the man of the previous moment: the line drawing of Trumper jumping out to drive would remain for the next twenty-five years. Why?

In some respects, Bradman was an ideal sequel to Trumper. He followed in the same tradition of autodidactism. He was instinctively enterprising with the bat, innately modest in person. 'Australia has unearthed a champion, self-taught, with natural ability,' stated Clem Hill. 'But most of all, with his heart in the right place.' Trumper's daughter was even sought out for approval of Bradman's 1930 records. 'We think Bradman is marvellous,' she told newspapers. 'Mother is especially excited. She has watched Bradman's progress with pride.'

Yet partly because the parallel between Trumper and Jackson was already so robust, it grew simpler to define Trumper and Bradman by contradistinction. Trumper was the lyric, Bradman the epic; Trumper was the Athenian, Bradman the Spartan; Trumper's age was identified with Edwardian brio, Bradman's with Fordist productivity. In retrospect, Bradman tends to be sentimentally identified with the Depression. At least as he emerged, he associated more readily with the project of modernism: Bradman 'the record breaker'; Bradman 'the run machine'. In the interwar years, Australians took pride in the maturation of their industries and expansion of their markets. Bradman radiated a comparable industrial efficiency, his statistics homologous with human progress and national potential.

Cricket, however, was a game, its heritage commonly seen as pastoral, its relations conservative, its inclinations romantic, its time spans long and gradual – it embraced rational and positivistic ends uneasily. Stupendous scores on doped wickets in the 1920s, when Victoria twice exceeded 1000 and Bill Ponsford twice exceeded 400, had already caused mutterings. 'This is the age of machinery,' protested Pelham Warner, 'but you cannot turn such a beautiful and subtle game as cricket into an affair of machinery.' Monty Noble saw the public succumbing to statistical delusions: 'Nowadays, far more notice is taken of batting averages than is good for the game. It is not how many runs a man makes, but how he makes them.' Bradman, then, occasioned immediate misgivings. When a 'correspondent from the country' asked him to rank Trumper and Bradman in *The Sun* in October 1930, Arthur Mailey described their eras as too difficult to compare, but left little doubt about his preference: 'It is fashionable now to break records. Ponsford started it and Bradman is finishing it with a vengeance. Bradman could never do the things Trumper did, and Trumper probably never wanted to do the things Bradman is doing.' He accepted Bradman haltingly: 'Trumper's batting was refined, cultured, and never undignified. Some of Bradman's strokes are crude by comparison, but, perhaps, more effective. The value of a batsman depends, I suppose, on the number of runs he scores. When making comparisons under the heading of value we must sacrifice artistry and grace for effectiveness.' *Perhaps. I suppose. The heading of value.* The concessions to modernity were grudging, and the issue, as Mailey acknowledged, ultimately evaded: 'Trumper was satisfied with a century. Bradman is not. That makes Bradman a more valuable batsman, but not greater, than Trumper. I am doubtful whether I have answered my country friend's question satisfactorily, but giving it in tabloid fashion I might say that Victor Trumper was a great batsman and Donald Bradman is a great run-getter.'

Bradman brought out, in fact, a certain unevolved Victorianism in cricket's aesthetic. His scores, huge, repetitive, homogenous, seemed distastefully out of proportion, almost inhuman: had Ruskin not warned that 'to banish imperfection is to destroy expression, to check exertion, to paralyse vitality'? Confronted by the objective reality of Bradman's runs, an elite of critics found grounds for subjective dispute, reasserting other criteria of evaluation: beauty, audacity, capacity in adversity, skill on poor wickets. Bradman quickly overshadowed Trumper's runs and steadily occluded his reputation. Yet in another respect, Bradman also ensured Trumper a continued relevance, as a counterpoint, as an alternative.

Unease around Bradman was not confined to his batting; his individualism disturbed the hard-won *status quo ante* of players and administrators. His profile and commercial heft soon rivalled the game's. The Board of Control looked askance at a twenty-two-year-old publishing his life story, especially as the serialisation of *Don Bradman's Book* (1930) in London's *Star* breached the clause of his tour contract forbidding 'any work for, or in connection with, any newspaper' – their decision to dock Bradman a third of his tour fee's 'good conduct' bonus, £50, presaged tense relations with cricket's new star. Needless to say, there was widespread public support for Bradman in the dispute – after all, he was the hero of the hour. But for those who wished to find fault, Trumper's legendary reticence and unworldliness offered a comparative standard. None observed the irony of Trumper's image adorning the publication of the association that had once suspended him; nobody wished to be reminded that Trumper had refused to tour England rather than accept the board's dictates. For this process was less about Trumper than it was about Bradman, whose relations with administration deteriorated so markedly over the next two years that he publicly countenanced abandoning the game in order to honour a contract to write for Associated Newspapers. In October 1932, Australian cricket faced a crisis the like of which it had not experienced in two decades.

Deep-seated misgivings about Bradman now found expression in a four-part series in the *Sydney Mail*, ostensibly adjudicating 'The Greatest Batsman of All Time'. Author Eric Barbour had been the finest flower of Sydney private school cricket before the war, scoring nearly 10 000 runs and taking nearly 500 wickets for Sydney Grammar, where his father George had been headmaster. George had also had a stint as Board of Control chairman, making close friends of establishment figures such as J. C. Davis and Frank Iredale, and Eric had imbibed many of their attitudes to amateurism and commercialisation. After the war he had put a medical career ahead of adding to a score of first-class matches, becoming instead a respected cricket pundit and pedagogue. His coaching manual, *The Making of a Cricketer* (1926), exhorted students of the game to be 'clean-living, clean-thinking and clean-talking'.

In the first three instalments of his series, Barbour ran the rule over Bradman, Trumper and W. G. Grace. While loyally saluting Bradman's run-scoring feats, Barbour deprecated his style: 'He plays many shots with a cross-bat; he frequently drives off his right foot; his defensive play, especially on the leg stump, is cramped and ungraceful.' Barbour ascribed this enunciation of 'efficiency, not artistry' to Bradman's rural upbringing, which had deprived his batting of metropolitan burnishing:

> Don Bradman grew up in a country centre, never saw Trumper bat, and did not see Kippax until he was himself a member of the N.S.W. side. His style has had to be his own, formed by experience

THE SYDNEY MAIL, WEDNESDAY, OCTOBER 12, 1932.—Page 8

Victor Trumper: "The grace and beauty of his stroke play have never been equalled by any other player." — Dr. E. Barbour.

Photograph by George Beldam, by courtesy of Mr. W. A. Oldfield.

# "The Greatest Batsman of All Time"

## Victor Trumper

### By Dr. Eric Barbour

VICTOR THOMAS TRUMPER was born at Sydney on November 2, 1877, and died on June 28, 1915, in his thirty-eighth year. Some of the members of our present Australian eleven were not even old enough to be taken to see him bat, but those of us who had the inestimable privilege of seeing him and playing with him in his prime will keep his memory green till the Great Umpire has sent the last of us to join him in the pavilion.

EDUCATED at Crown-street school, Trumper in his boyhood showed a natural grace of style and a degree of skill that perhaps was not as rapidly recognised in those days as it would be to-day. In 1897 his appearance in Sydney grade cricket, or electorate cricket as it was then called, was an auspicious opening for a phenomenal career, for in eight innings, three of which were not out, he compiled the amazing aggregate of 1021 runs. J. R. M. Mackay exceeded this in 1905-06 with 1041, but had thirteen innings, and of those who have since then reached the thousand mark Bardsley had fifteen innings and Andrews seventeen. The first indication that the outer world had of the appearance of a new star in its firmament was in 1894, when he scored 292 against Tasmania and followed it with 253 against New Zealand. But this shy and unobtrusive youngster then found, as others had found before him, that to break into the Australian eleven was about as difficult a job as cracking a Bank of England safe. It was only the power of public opinion that forced him into the 1899 team for England as fourteenth man. Those who wished to exclude him must subsequently have looked foolish, for from the time of his arrival in England he began a career of meteoric brilliance that has made him the most pictu-resque figure in the history of Australian cricket and the most gifted exponent of the batsman's art that the world has ever seen.

NOT that his greatness was always reflected in actual figures; there are many, both in England and in Australia, whose figures, over a long period, are superior to those of Trumper. He had his good seasons

> The three articles which have traced the careers of Don Bradman, the late Dr. Grace, and the late Victor Trumper will be followed by a fourth, to be published next week. It will be a summing up, and we think that no cricketer will challenge the conclusions of Dr. Eric Barbour as to which of the three is entitled to be regarded as "The Greatest Batsman of All Time" and the relative positions occupied by the others.

and his lean seasons but, whatever his results, he was always the "Nonpareil," the unequalled. To-day is the material age of figures and records. In cricket, athletics, swimming, and horse-racing we see the same tendency. Trumper lived and played in days when no one, least of all Trumper himself, bothered his head about records, aggregates, or averages. Almost invariably he threw his innings away after reaching a century, and often were before, if the winning of the match for his side were not in question. He played cricket first and foremost for the joy of it; he loved the thrill of cracking the ball like a pistol shot, and the exultation of daring and seemingly impossible shots lured him more than the size of his score. A batsman so adventurous, so care-free, and so regardless of the scoring book could not avoid frequent failures; but even his failures were greater than most men's successes, for twenty runs from Trumper remained in the memory longer than a hundred from most of his contemporaries. I shall quote a few of his outstanding performances, beginning with the 1899 tour of England. On this tour, although he just struggled into the side, he was third in the aggregates with 1556 runs. His 135 not out in the Lord's test set all England talking, and he followed it with 300 not out against Sussex, the record score for an Australian in England at that period. Returning to Australia, a score of 230 against Victoria was his most notable contribution in the following year, when he again headed the aggregates in Sydney grade cricket.

HIS triumphal tour of England in 1902 must rank as the peak period of his career. In one of the wettest summers on record he scored 2570 runs, including eleven centuries. What the size of his aggregate could have been had he wished we can only conjecture, for of his eleven centuries the highest score was 128, and regularly he threw his wicket away after reaching three figures. The speed of his scoring and the artistry of his stroke play amazed the English critics, who lost no time in enthroning him in place of their erstwhile idol, Ranjitsinhji. In a succession of innings, of which every one was a gem, it is not easy to select the greatest, but some of them may be mentioned. In the historic fourth test at Manchester, dramatically won by Australia by a margin of three runs, Trumper opened with a glorious 104, on a wicket soft after rain, and, as Wisden relates, "without a mistake of any kind."

### A Triumphal Tour

'The Greatest': Barbour's Trumper.

and tested by results. The unprecedented success that has come to him is a wonderful tribute to the mind that devised it. Indeed, there will be many who will say that if Bradman's style differs from that of the old masters, then the old masters must have been wrong. Without subscribing to such bolshevism, we can at least pay the tribute of admiration to this extraordinary youngster, who from his cricketing cradle has done everything for himself and has achieved such marvellous results.

The rub was revealed when Barbour considered Bradman in relation to the board. While Barbour approved Bradman's 'quiet philosophic detachment' and 'inscrutable smile', he regretted that Bradman had 'shown the tendency to commercialise his outstanding success to a degree that has not been attempted by any of his predecessors in Australian cricket'. This was 'hardly in keeping with cricket tradition'; indeed, it smacked of the 'professionalism' tainting rugby league:

> There are many hundreds of people, some closely associated with the game, who are only too ready to give the wrong advice to a young player on these matters; many of them will say, 'Get as much out of it as you can while the going is good; cricket will not keep you when you are old and stiff.' But there are many thousands who think differently, and they include practically all the real men of Australian cricket. Cricket, fortunately, is not yet in the position of League football, nor do we wish it to be . . . The essential point is that no player is greater than the game itself, and it is unfair for any one player to be treated differently from others merely because his performances are greater.

On the issue of Bradman's present stand-off, Barbour opined that the board had dallied too long, but also that its stipulations required compliance – for him a conclusion rooted in filial piety. 'The Board of Control has for many years had the sympathy and support of the majority of the cricket-lovers of New South Wales,' he recalled. 'They stood behind it in that most critical year of 1913 [sic], when the point at issue was whether the game should control the players or the players the game . . . Criticise it as we will, there is no denying the fact that the Board is the governing body and its decisions must stand.' The more so, Barbour felt, because the board formed a rampart against vulgarising, American-accented materialism:

> Cricket is either a game or a business. If it is a game, let it be managed and administered as a game, and kept in the proud position it has occupied for so many years. If it is going to degenerate into a business, with the moral standards and box-office criteria of Hollywood or the Chicago White Sox, let us admit it forthwith and have an immediate choice by every player between amateurism and professionalism.
>
> I am aware that many will contend that this digression is beside the point when discussing the greatness of a batsman; my own view is that the personal factor must be considered, as the attitude of a player to the game may have a great bearing on the comparative value of his performances. Further, the question of example for young players must be taken into consideration, for the greatest batsman of the day can do no wrong in the eyes of the younger generation.

Writing a fortnight later of Trumper, Barbour left all the foregoing out of account. Trumper's belief in the players' entitlement to the spoils of Ashes tours; Trumper's distaste for and resistance of the Board of Control; even Trumper's involvement in the foundation of barbarous rugby league: all these were forgotten. Instead, Barbour appropriated Trumper for amateurism. 'He played cricket first and foremost for the joy of it; he loved the thrill of cracking the ball like a pistol shot, and the exultation of daring and seemingly impossible shots lured him more than the size of his score,' claimed Barbour.

> A batsman so adventurous, so carefree, and so regardless of the scoring book could not avoid frequent failures; but even his failures were greater than most men's successes, for twenty runs from Trumper remained in the memory longer than a hundred from most of his contemporaries. I am quite sure that to him cricket was not nearly so serious a business as it is to the modern young man. It is impossible to measure the achievements of an artist by statistics and records.

In conclusion, Barbour argued against 'the material age of figures and records', confident that others shared his views: Bradman's 'quiet certainty and confidence' did not 'inspire the warm affection that seemed to belong to Trumper' with his 'easy-going and good-natured' character. Readers would have felt no surprise at Barbour's eventual conclusion: 'I am sufficiently old-fashioned to look upon batsmanship as primarily an art, and for that reason I still regard Victor Trumper in his prime as the greatest batsman that ever lived.' Perhaps in anticipation of disagreement, Barbour had recourse to Noble's old observation that Trumper had to be seen: 'Some of the members of our present Australian eleven were not even old enough to be taken to see him bat, but those of us who had the inestimable privilege of seeing him and playing with him in his prime will keep his memory green till the Great Umpire has sent the last of us to join him in the pavilion.' For those deprived of that 'inestimable privilege', evidence was provided: a reproduction of 'Jumping Out', this time borrowed from Bert Oldfield's sports store.

Though crisis was averted when Associated Newspapers waived its contract for Bradman's services, still graver events were in the offing. Two weeks after Barbour resolved to his own satisfaction that batting was an art, Marylebone arrived for a tour that made it look more of an ordeal. The Bodyline series would reset relations between the countries, leave Oldfield with a fractured skull, and Barbour with fractured ideals. With Alan Kippax, he poured his grievances into a screed, *Anti-Bodyline* (1933), denigrating the 'Bodyliner' as 'on par with a footballer who puts the boot in' – a scathing appraisal of England's amateur captain Douglas Jardine. By then, too, Barbour was facing deliberation of the Great Umpire, in the form of the colon cancer that killed him in January 1934.[*]

It was a challenging time to love cricket, as Richard Binns worried in *Cricket in Firelight*: 'The survivors of a period which did so much to raise cricket to its highest levels must, like ourselves, be concerned for the future well-being of the game. No sensitive cricketer's ear can be deaf to the harsh notes that have crept into the harmony of cricket during the last two or three years . . . which need to be resolved.' For one writer, such assuagement was a long-term project.

•

If not the solo inventor of 'the Golden Age' as a descriptor of cricket before World War I, Neville Cardus was, as it were, its patron.

---

[*] Trumper appears to have sustained Barbour to the last: his final published work, printed posthumously by the *Sydney Mail* in February 1935, was a further lengthy tribute to his hero: 'Bat Magic: The Art of Victor Trumper'.

Most writers slip into nostalgia only as their careers evolve. Cardus was rheumy-eyed almost as soon as his career began, even about cricket he had not seen. The opening chapter of his first book, *A Cricketer's Book* (1922), recounts arriving early for an Australian practice session at Lord's and slipping into 'a reverie' of 'the great days of cricket' – specifically the inaugural Ashes Test of 1882, six years before his birth:

> I lost grip on events. It seemed that I sat there till the ground was
> almost deserted, till over the field came a faint mist, and with it
> the vague melancholy of twilight in a great city. Time to go home,
> I thought ... a great match ... great days ... great men ... all
> gone ... far away ... departed glory ... A hand of someone touched
> my shoulder and I heard him say: 'The Orsetralians are on the way,
> and they'll be in the nets at four o'clock. Nice in the sun, isn't it?'

*Departed glory*: a common sensation in postwar England, and Cardus knew how to sheet blame home. It was the waning of amateur influence that had left cricket 'steeped neck-high in mediocrity' and under the sway of his archetypal lookalike professional 'Bloggs of Blankshire'. What a contrast to the cricket of before the war, so 'symbolical of the age's prestige'. What a contrast to Trumper: 'The manly chivalry of Victor Trumper, whose bat was always a banner in the air, will move us like poetry long after his performances have been buried out of sight under the dump of statistics which summer by summer are piled up prodigiously.' Unlike Binns and Carew, Cardus seldom addressed war directly; nor, unlike such belletrists of ruralism as E. V. Lucas and A. G. Macdonell, did he identify cricket with a village idyll. But his longing for a better time, a pristine bygone age of pedigreed amateurs and yeoman professionals, became an analog of national decline, disillusion and loss.

Cardus first gave this better time a name, tentatively and without capitalisation, in an elegy of Trumper in *The Guardian* on 24 July 1926: 'Trumper's winged batsmanship was seen in the golden age of cricket; he was, at his finest, master of some of the greatest bowlers the game has ever known.' Most readers would have understood the concept instinctively. The British Empire claimed a sort of lineal descent from great days past, from 'golden ages' of Greece and Rome. Not long before, too, Britain had attempted to roll back time by returning the Empire to the gold standard – a disastrous caprice that rendered much imperial industry uncompetitive by bloating the value of sterling, but which enjoyed popular appeal as an assertion of economic virility. Cardus had not sole licence on the expression 'golden age', which enjoyed a number of variations around this time. But only he applied it so sweepingly, and with such occasionally magisterial condescension.

'It is not the fault of the professionals that since the War they have not had before them the example of amateur style as we knew it in the golden age,' Cardus claimed in *Cricket* (1930), his contribution to Longmans' English Heritage Series. 'But the professional batsman in the lump, despite a superb and honourable skill, too often lets us know from his cricket that he learned to play in a world where a drab struggle went on persistently, and where every penny had to be hoarded, and where to be spendthrift was to be a sinner.' Trumper, by comparison, was 'enrobed in purple', 'a conquistador', 'a Saladin cleaving the silken cushion with his scimitar'. And just in case this was thought fanciful, Cardus flourished the most modern of empirical proofs: 'Look at the photographs of him, doubting young Thomases of the skeptical present, and see how far he would venture beyond the crease's rim at the sight of a well-tossed ball; his bat is held up behind him punitively, he is leaping to the ball, his every muscle responding to the demands of the will to power and victory.'

By the mid-1930s, Cardus was regularly capitalising 'Golden Age'; by decade's end, he was effectively quoting himself, referring to 'the period which I call the Golden Age of cricket', glow furbished by 'the genius of Trumper', connection reinforced by auto-biographical recollections. And of the pantheon of cricket divinities that Cardus stocked to evoke his lost England, Trumper is the most interestingly perdurable, being from furthest away, and by springing straight from the writer's youth actually prefiguring many of the preferences he later formed, such as for the cricket of the public schools, for the abiding rivalry of Yorkshire v Lancashire, and for the civilising influence of Tonbridge's nursery of batsmanship. By dying almost simultaneously with the advent of the war that ended the Golden Age, Trumper also became its ideal personification, while his lingering ill-health could act as a metaphor of the era's fragile, doomed beauty.

The greater the loss and isolation, the brighter the past burned. It was in *English Cricket* (1945), a monograph written for William Collins' morale-boosting 'Britain in Pictures' series during his war-time sojourn in Sydney, that Cardus argued most fervently for 'the mighty convulsion of energy of genius which, between 1890 and 1914, hurled up all the peaks, the mighty ranges on which repose in unap-proachable grandeur the masters of the Golden Age of Cricket'. Since then, thanks to the dwindling ranks of 'amateur players from the old social mint', the game had petrified under the sway of 'robot batsmen' involved in 'mechanical run-making'. Bradman? Cardus appreciated his 'spifflication of all bowling', but without the effusive warmth he reserved for Trumper: 'Efficiency, superb stream-lined efficiency! And don't mistake me, Bradman is often grand and exhilarating to watch. But if I were asked to compare him with Trumper I should say the difference is as that between the flight of the aeroplane and the flight of an eagle.' So while others rehearsed these themes, none couched them as persuasively or eulogistically as cricket's *homo aestheticus*, or condensed them to a phrase that tripped from the tongue so readily.

So captivating was the idea, in fact, that by the 1960s a wistful historicising of 'the Golden Age of Cricket' had begun, reinforced in books bearing the title by A. A. Thomson (1961), Patrick Morrah (1967) and Robert Trumble (1968). With the abolition of amateur status, cricket was losing its last connection to the idea of a gentlemanly vanguard. The trauma of war had given way to a more manageable but deeper ache. 'Of course, most of us have our own private Golden Ages, to which we look back as if remembering a lost world,' wrote J. B. Priestley, then in his late eighties, in the foreword to David Frith's *The Golden Age of Cricket* (1981). 'My own is roughly from 1910 to 1914, when I joined the Army and began to lose so many friends, when I entered another world, *which could never again be trusted* . . . Golden Ages, however different in other respects, have this in common: they will soon come to an end.' And when this particular *belle époque* needed to be reduced to a single image, there was only one for which to reach.

# 10

# 'WHAT A
# LOVELY PICTURE!'

'On all the walls of all leading cricket club rooms there hangs
a picture, a picture of a batsman sweeping a ball to leg [sic], and beneath
it a simple plaque bearing the name "Victor Trumper".'
– 'Victor Trumper', episode of radio serial
*They Were Champions*, 3DB, 19 December 1953

In January 1947, the *Sydney Morning Herald* reported the death of
Lock Walmsley, president of the Sydney Musicians' Club, whose
orchestras had been playing old-time dance tunes in halls and cinemas
since before World War I. A much-loved character, he had prolonged
his penchant for the last word beyond death by recording his will on a
gramophone disc so 'they can't argue about that'. Having thus appor-
tioned his assets, Walmsley decided that he had one further thing

to add: 'I would like to record for posterity that Victor Trumper was the best batsman of the lot.' With that he proceeded to his grave.

For the demographic front was moving ineluctably. As Australia hosted England that summer in the first postwar Ashes series, barely a quarter of Australia's population were old enough to have first-hand recollection of Trumper. Those who still remembered did so ardently. During the Second Test in Sydney, England's Len Hutton played a brief, blazing innings of 37 in twenty-four minutes that brought the Hill to its feet. 'Those who were lucky enough to see this remarkable display must have grieved with me that such a super-lative innings was nipped in its golden prime,' wrote the *Herald*'s Bill O'Reilly. Not long afterwards, Hutton received a lengthy letter, signed simply 'Aussie', which he cherished evermore:

> Dear Sir,
>
> Both for myself and for a number of my Australian friends I want to extend to you our gratitude for the truly grand innings you played in England's second knock. It was a delight to the connoisseur of batsmanship, and brought to us again visions of the peerless Trumper, whom we saw in many of his matchless innings . . . Trumper was a glorious batsman, the acme of consummate grace and beauty when at his best – the gay cavalier of cricket, playing for sheer love of the game, his rapier-like bat flashing in carefree abandon and loveliness. Bradman does not compare with him as an artist.

Such aficionados were also conscious of their outnumbering. Revered former teammates like Noble, Darling, Trumble, Hill and Laver; journalists who had tended the Trumper legend such as Davis, Horan, Barbour, Poidevin, Knight, Trevor: all were gone by the time 'Aussie' sent his letter. Twenty years after Ben Travers had seen an SCG member decried for the blasphemy of comparing Bradman to Trumper, *Sporting Globe*'s Hec de Lacy sat in a crowd at the MCG during Bradman's testimonial match experiencing the opposite sensation:

> I saw both Trumper and Bradman, Trumper perhaps at that teen age when impressions and convictions are absorbed more readily than in the cold light of middle age. The superlative ease and grace with which Trumper did everything has often made me say of other champions, 'He's great, but he's no Trumper.' But for the life of me, I can't persuade my sons to accept Trumper, as I accept Trumper. Neither can any other father. Generations of cricketers are apart, and youth lives in the ever-bright present.

How, then, to revive Trumper for an audience that had mostly never seen him? Bradman was the game's benchmark, in quality and quantity. He had minted runs in such abundance as to be comparable only to himself, relegating Trumper's statistics almost to a historical footnote.

Nor were there heirs to anoint, no Kippaxes or Jacksons to speak of. The best that de Lacy's *Sporting Globe* could do, for example, was two teenagers. Vic Michael and Ray Flockton, two years apart, shattered school cricket records left and right in the late 1940s, but it was their provenance that attracted attention: they were alumni of Trumper's Crown Street School.* Both became useful cricketers; neither was a natural legatee of Trumper's. A 'new Trumper' was arguably less likely than a 'new Bradman'.

---

* Ray Flockton played thirty-seven first-class matches for New South Wales averaging 41; Vic Michael made 3735 first-grade runs for St George averaging 26.

the philanthropic spirit of Steve Waugh,' Strange told the *Sydney Morning Herald*. 'I suppose for Queenslanders like myself,' said Prime Minister Kevin Rudd on dedicating the Trumper Stand in December 2008, 'Trumper could be best described as a combination of Wally Lewis, John Eales, Michael Voss and Matthew Hayden.' But Rudd then seemed to realise that he had no need of such lumpy mash-ups. 'The Trumper legend for later generations is grounded in that great black-and-white photograph of him launching that powerful Trumper drive,' he stated. 'You *know* that photograph. It just sits in your mind and your memory.' And he was right.

•

The day before the Fifth Test of the Ashes of 2015, I spent part of the afternoon with photographer Philip Brown dodging about the outfield at The Oval, him with his camera, me with a vintage survey map of Kennington from London Metropolitan Archives and a copy of 'Jumping Out', in search of the same vantage as Beldam in 1905. Inevitably the backdrop had changed. The terraces of what was now called the Peter May Stand stretched unbroken. Thirty years after Beldam's visit, the Clayton Arms had been demolished for the social housing today called Kennington Park Estate; the pub had crossed to the other side of the road, been renamed The Cricketers in 1966, and lain derelict since its closure ten years earlier.

Yet Clayton Street stretched in the same direction, opening the same gap in the skyline. Refurbished as apartments, the building that once housed the Kennington Road School, visible in the far distance of 'Jumping Out', still stood; likewise the great gasometers. And between times the pitch square at The Oval had not budged an inch. At its eastern extremity, as we watched, Steve Smith was immersed in a session of throwdowns on more or less the spot where Trumper and Beldam had rendezvoused eleven decades earlier; when we returned from exploring the pavilion half an hour later, in fact, Australia's captain-to-be was still hard at work. We left him at it. The following day he made a hundred.

Has Smith heard of Victor Trumper, I wondered? Possibly. George Beldam? Definitely not. Never mind: he sort of knows them anyway.

Next man in: The Oval, 2015.

Three biographies have been published of Victor Trumper: Jack Fingleton's *The Immortal Victor Trumper* (Collins, London, 1978), Ashley Mallett's *Trumper: The Illustrated Biography* (Macmillan, South Melbourne, 1985) and Peter Sharpham's *Trumper: The Definitive Biography* (Hodder & Stoughton, Sydney, 1985). Fingleton's working materials are at the State Library of NSW, MLMSS 5691/Box 21; the uncorrected proof referred to in the text was provided by Russell Jackson; David Frith was kind enough to send me his lengthy corrections, and also to draw my attention to Trumper's correspondence with Worcestershire CCC.

A fourth most useful compilation was published on the centenary of Trumper's death collating papers delivered at a seminar on his life, edited by its organiser, Ronald Cardwell. Particularly useful in *The Life and Times of the Immortal Victor Trumper* (Cricket Publishing Company, Sydney, 2015) are the contributions of Alf James and Jim Cattlin concerning Trumper's junior and grade cricket, and Cardwell's own analysis of Trumper's business career, but everything is readable and illuminating.

Particular of Trumper's feats and fortunes have inspired other works: Lionel H. Brown's *Victor Trumper and the 1902 Australians* (Secker & Warburg, London, 1981), John Hawkins' *Trumper's Team in Queensland 1906* (Christopher Saunders, Newnham on Severn, 2012), Gerry Wolstenholme's *Trumper Triumphant: His Final*

*First-class Century in England, Blackpool 1909* (Red Rose Books, Bolton, 2002), and a compilation of newspaper articles about his last big innings, *Great Knock: Sim's Australians v. Canterbury, played at Lancaster Park, Christchurch, 27, 28 February, 2 March 1914* (Nag's Head Press, Christchurch, 1978). Trumper provides numerous chapters in various edited compilations, those of special note being Neville Cardus's appreciation in John Arlott's *Cricket: The Great Ones* (Pelham, London, 1967), and Ross McMullin's in Garrie Hutchinson's *Test Team of the Century* (HarperSports, Sydney, 2000).

George Beldam can claim principal ownership of the following works:

*Great Golfers: Their Methods at a Glance* (notes by Harry Vardon, James Braid, Alexander Herd, J. H. Taylor), Macmillan, London, 1904

*Golf Faults Illustrated* (with J. H. Taylor), George Newnes Ltd, London, 1904

*Great Lawn Tennis Players: Their Methods Illustrated* (with P. A. Vaile), Macmillan, London, 1905

*Great Batsmen: Their Methods at a Glance* (with C. B. Fry), Macmillan, London, 1905

*Great Bowlers and Fielders: Their Methods at a Glance* (with C. B. Fry, F. R. Spofforth, B. J. T. Bosanquet, R. O. Schwarz), Macmillan, London, 1906

*Cricket Illustrated*, Gowans & Gray, London, 1908

*Golfing Illustrated*, Gowans & Gray, London, 1908

*The World's Champion Golfers: Their Art Disclosed by the Ultra-Rapid Camera*, Photochrome Co. Ltd, London, 1924 (11 volumes)

Beldam also provided illustrations for:

Vaile, Percy A., *Modern Lawn Tennis: Illustrated by Explanatory Diagrams and by Action Photographs Taken Expressly for This Work*, William Heinemann, London, 1904

Tayler, A. Chevallier, *The Empire's Cricketers: Season 1905*, Fine Art Society, London, 1905

Broadbent Trowsdale, T., *The Cricketers' Autograph Birthday Book*, Walter Scott Publishing Company, London, 1906

Watts, Mrs Roger, *The Fine Art of Jujutsu*, William Heinemann, London, 1906

Duncan, George and Bernard Darwin, *Present-day Golf*, Hodder & Stoughton, 1921

Fry, S. H., *Billiards for Amateurs*, Hodder & Stoughton, London, 1922

The indispensable volume on Beldam's life and work, mentioned in the text, is *Great Cricketers: The Age of Grace & Trumper* (Boundary Books, Goostrey, 2000), compiled by George Beldam Jnr and edited by his widow, Cornelia. Beldam gave a professional appraisal of his work in an interview with Adolphe Abrahams in a series, 'Sports and the Camera', for *The Photographic News* (21 June 1907) and a historical analysis of batsmanship in 'Style and Progression: Influences at Work in the Batsman's Art', a chapter in *British Sports and Sportsmen: Cricket and Football* (*The Sportsman*, London 1917, pp. 100–09). Further biographical information is from 'A Chat with Mr G. W. Beldam' in *Cricket: A Weekly Record of the Game* (20 June 1901) and 'A Full Innings' by Roy Beldam in the *Peterhouse Annual Record 2005/6* (University of Cambridge), pp. 45–53.

# CRICKET: BIOGRAPHY AND AUTOBIOGRAPHY

Batchelor, Denzil, *C. B. Fry*, Phoenix House, London, 1951

Bonnell, Max, *Currency Lads: The Life and Cricket of T. W. Garrett,
R. C. Allen, S. P. Jones and R. J. Pope*, Cricket Publishing Company,
Cherrybrook, 2001

Booth, Keith, *The Father of Modern Sport: The Life and Times
of Charles W. Alcock*, Parrs Wood Press, Manchester, 2002

Bradman, Donald, *Don Bradman's Book: The Story of My Cricketing Life
to August 1930*, Hutchinson, London, 1931

Bradman, Donald, *Farewell to Cricket*, Hodder & Stoughton,
London, 1950

Brodribb, Gerald, *The Croucher: A Biography of Gilbert Jessop*,
London Magazine Editions, London, 1974

Brookes, Christopher, *His Own Man: The Life of Neville Cardus*,
Unwin Paperbacks, London, 1986

Cardus, Neville, *Autobiography*, Collins, London, 1947

Cardus, Neville, *Second Innings*, Collins, London, 1950

Cardus, Neville, *Full Score*, Cassell, London, 1970

Cashman, Richard, *The 'Demon' Spofforth*, UNSW Press,
Kensington, 1990

Daft, Richard, *Kings of Cricket: Reminiscences and Anecdotes, with Hints
on the Game*, Arrowsmith, Bristol, 1893

Daft, Richard, *A Cricketer's Yarns*, Chapman & Hall, London, 1926

Daniels, Robin, *Conversations with Cardus*, Gollancz, London, 1976

Darling, D. K., *Test Tussles On and Off the Field*, self-published,
Hobart, 1970

Down, Michael, *Archie: A Biography of A. C. MacLaren*, Allen & Unwin,
London, 1981

Ellis, Clive, *C. B.: The Life of Charles Burgess Fry*, Dent, London, 1984

Fingleton, Jack, *Batting from Memory*, Collins, London, 1981

Furniss, Harry, E. J. Milliken and E. B. V. Christian, *A Century of Grace*, Bristol, 1896

Frith, David, *Archie Jackson: The Keats of Cricket*, Pavilion, London, 1987

Frith, David, *Caught England, Bowled Australia: A Cricket Slave's Complex Story*, Eva Press, London, 1997

Fry, C. B., *Life Worth Living*, Eyre & Spottiswoode, London, 1939

Grace, W. G., *Cricket*, Arrowsmith, Bristol, 1891

Haigh, Gideon, *The Big Ship: Warwick Armstrong and the Making of Modern Cricket*, Text Publishing, Melbourne, 2001

Hill, Les, *Eighty Not Out: The Story of W. J. (Bill) Whitty of Tantanoola*, Laurie & Watson, Mount Gambier, 1966

Hutton, Len, *Cricket Is My Life*, Hutchinson & Co., London, 1949

Iredale, Frank, *33 Years of Cricket*, Beatty, Richardson & Co., Sydney, 1920

Jessop, Gilbert, *A Cricketer's Log*, Hodder & Stoughton, London, 1922

Laver, Frank, *An Australian Cricketer on Tour*, Bell, London, 1905

Lilley, A. A., *Twenty-four Years of Cricket*, Mills & Boon, London, 1912

Macartney, Charles, *My Cricketing Days*, William Heinemann, London, 1930

McCool, Colin, *Cricket Is a Game*, Stanley Paul, London, 1961

Mailey, Arthur, *10 for 66 and All That*, Phoenix Sports Books, London, 1958

Mitchell, Alan, *84 Not Out: The Story of Sir Arthur Sims, Kt*, Hennel Locke, London, 1962

Monfries, J. Elliott, *Not Test Cricket*, Gillingham, Adelaide, 1950

Moyes, A. G., *Bradman*, Angus & Robertson, Sydney, 1948

Myers, A. Wallis, *C. B. Fry: The Man and His Methods*, J. W. Arrowsmith, Bristol, 1912

Rae, Simon, *W. G. Grace: A Life*, Faber & Faber, London, 1998

Raiji, Vasant, *Ranji: The Legend and the Man*, self-published, Bombay, 1963

Raiji, Vasant (ed.), *Victor Trumper: The Beau Ideal of a Cricketer,* Vivek, Bombay, 1964

Root, Fred, *A Cricket Pro's Lot,* Edward Arnold, London, 1937

Rosenwater, Irving, *Sir Donald Bradman,* Batsford, London, 1978

Sissons, Ric, *Reggie: Five Years of Fame – The Story of Reginald Duff,* Cricket Publishing Company, Sydney, 2016

Tomlinson, Richard, *Amazing Grace: The Man who Was W. G.,* Little, Brown, London, 2015

Travers, Ben, *94 Declared,* Elm Tree Books, London, 1981

Trumble, Robert, *The Golden Age of Cricket,* self-published, Melbourne, 1968

Whimpress, Bernard (ed.), *Clem Hill's Reminiscences: The 'Unwritten History' of His Test Career, 1896–1912,* Association of Cricket Statisticians & Historians, Cardiff, 2007

Wilde, Simon, *Ranji: A Genius Rich and Strange,* Kingswood, London, 1999

Wilton, Iain, *C. B. Fry: An English Hero,* Richard Cohen, London, 1999

Wright, L. G., *Scraps from a Cricketer's Memory,* Derbyshire County Cricket Supporters Club, Derbyshire, 1980

## CRICKET: HISTORY

Alcock, Charles and Lord Alverstone (eds), *Surrey Cricket: Its History and Associations,* Longmans, Green, London, 1902

Altham, H. S., and E. W. Swanton, *A History of Cricket,* 2nd edition, George Allen & Unwin, London, 1938

Bateman, Anthony, *Cricket, Literature and Culture: Symbolising the Nation, Destabilising Empire,* Ashgate Publishing, Farnham, 2009

Bonnell, Max and James Rodgers, *Golden Blues: Sydney University Cricket – 150 Years of the Club and Its Players,* Darlington Press, Sydney, 2014

Cannane, Steve, *First Tests: Great Australian Cricketers and the Backyards that Made Them*, ABC Books, Sydney, 2009

Chignell, W. R., *A History of the Worcestershire County Cricket Club*, Littlebury & Co., London, 1951

Derriman, Phil, *True to the Blue: A History of the New South Wales Cricket Association*, Richard Smart Publishing, Sydney, 1985

Fahey, Michael and Mike Coward, *The Baggy Green: The Pride, Passion and History of Australia's Sporting Icon*, Cricket Publishing Company, West Pennant Hills, 2008

Frith, David, *The Trailblazers: The First English Cricket Tour of Australia, 1861–62*, Boundary Books, Cheshire, 1999

Green, Benny, *A History of Cricket*, Barrie & Jenkins, London, 1988

Haigh, Gideon and David Frith, *Inside Story: Unlocking Australian Cricket's Archives*, News Custom Publishing, Melbourne, 2007

Howat, Gerald, *Cricket's Second Golden Age*, Hodder & Stoughton, London, 1989

Kynaston, David, *WG's Birthday Party*, Chatto & Windus, London, 1990

Lazenby, John, *The Strangers who Came Home: The First Australian Cricket Tour of England*, John Wisden & Co., London, 2015

Lemmon, David, *The Official History of Worcestershire County Cricket Club*, Christopher Helm, London, 1989

McCleary, G. F., *Cricket with the Kangaroo: Studies in Anglo-Australian Cricket*, Hollis & Carter, London, 1950

Mallett, Ashley, *Eleven: The Greatest Eleven of the 20th Century*, UQP, St Lucia, 2001

Montefiore, David, *Cricket in the Doldrums: The Struggle Between Private and Public Control of Australian Cricket in the 1880s*, Australian Society for Sports History, University of Western Sydney, 1992

Morrah, Patrick, *The Golden Age of Cricket*, Eyre & Spottiswoode, London, 1967

Moyes, A. G., *Australian Cricket: A History*, Angus & Robertson, Sydney, 1959

Mulvaney, John and Rex Harcourt, *Cricket Walkabout: The Australian Aborigines in England*, Macmillan, South Melbourne, 1988

Palgrave, Louis, *The Story of the Oval and the History of Surrey Cricket: 1902 to 1948*, Cornish Brothers, Birmingham, 1949

Parish, R. J., & ors (eds.), *Centenary Test Melbourne 12-17 March 1977: Official Souvenir Publication of the Australian Cricket Board*, Australian Cricket Board, Melbourne, 1977

Plumptre, George, *The Golden Age of Cricket*, Queen Anne Press, London, 1990

Pollard, Jack, *The Turbulent Years of Australian Cricket 1893–1917*, Angus & Robertson, Sydney, 1987

Ranjitsinhji, Kumar Shri, *With Stoddart's Team in Australia*, James Bowden, London, 1898

Robinson, Ray, *On Top Down Under*, Cassell Australia, Sydney, 1975

Sandiford, Keith, *Cricket and the Victorians*, Scolar Press, Aldershot, 1994

Sandiford, Keith and Brian Stoddart (eds), *The Imperial Game*, Manchester University Press, Manchester, 1998

Sharpham, Peter, *The 1899 Australians in England*, J. W. McKenzie, Epsom, 1997

Sissons, Ric, *The Players: A Social History of the Professional Cricketer*, Pluto Press, Sydney, 1988

Smith, Rick, *Cricket Brawl: The 1912 Dispute*, Apple Books, Launceston, 1995

Standing, Percy Cross, *Cricket of To-day and Yesterday*, Caxton, London, 1902

Warner, Pelham, *How We Recovered the Ashes*, Chapman and Hall, London, 1904

Whimpress, Bernard, *Passport to Nowhere: Aborigines in Australian Cricket 1850–1939*, Walla Walla Press, Sydney, 1999

Williams, Jack, *Cricket and England: A Cultural and Social History of the Inter-war Years*, Frank Cass, London, 1999

Winder, Robert, *The Little Wonder: The Remarkable History of Wisden*, Bloomsbury, London, 2013

Yapp, Nick, *A History of the Foster's Oval*, Pelham, London, 1990

## CRICKET: INSTRUCTION

Barbour, E. P., *The Making of a Cricketer*, Sydney & Melbourne Publishing Company, Sydney, 1926

Barnes, A. R, *Calling All Cricketers: A Cricket Coaching Manual*, NSW Cricket Association, Sydney, 1955, 1964

Benson, E. F. and Eustace H. Miles (eds), *The Cricket of Abel, Hirst, and Shrewsbury*, Hurst & Blackett, London, 1903

Bradman, Sir Donald, *The Art of Cricket*, Hodder & Stoughton, London, 1958

Felix, Nicholas, *Felix on the Bat: Being a Scientific Inquiry into the Use of the Cricket Bat; Together with the History and Use of the Catapulta*, Bally Bros, London, 1845

Fry, C. B., *Cricket (Batsmanship)*, Eveleigh, Nash & Grayson, London, 1912

Jessop, Gilbert, *Cricket and How to Play It*, Harrap, London, 1925

Marylebone Cricket Club, *The MCC Cricket Coaching Book*, The Naldrett Press in association with World's Work, Kingswood, 1955

Murdoch, W. L., *Cricket*, George Routledge, London, 1893

Noble, Monty, *The Game's the Thing*, Cassell, London, 1926

Nyren, John, *The Young Cricketer's Tutor and The Cricketers of My Time*, Effingham Wilson, London, 1833

Pollard, Jack (ed.), *Cricket, the Australian Way*, Lansdowne Press, Melbourne, 1961

Ranjitsinhji, Kumar Shri, *The Jubilee Book of Cricket*, Blackwood, Edinburgh, 1897

Rudd, Cecil and Edgar Witham, *Cricket for Boys*, James Nisbet, London, 1937

Steel, A. G., and R H. Lyttleton (eds.), *Cricket*, Badminton Library of Sports and Pastimes, Longmans, Green, London, 1888

Warner, Pelham (ed.), *Cricket: A New Edition*, Badminton Library of Sports and Pastimes, Longmans, Green, London, 1920

Warner, Pelham, *The Book of Cricket*, revised edition, J. M. Dent & Sons, London, 1922

## CRICKET: LITERATURE

Ashley-Cooper, F. S., *Cricket Highways and Byways*, George Allen & Unwin, London, 1927

Berry, Scyld, *Cricket: The Game of Life*, Hodder & Stoughton, London, 2015

Binns, Richard, *Cricket in Firelight*, Selwyn & Blount, London, 1935

Cardus, Neville, *A Cricketer's Book*, Grant Richards, London, 1922

Cardus, Neville, *Days in the Sun: A Cricketer's Journal*, Grant Richards, London, 1924

Cardus, Neville, *The Summer Game: A Cricketer's Journal*, Cayme Press, London, 1929

Cardus, Neville, *Cricket*, Longmans, Green, London, 1930

Cardus, Neville, *Good Days: A Book of Cricket*, Jonathan Cape, London, 1934

Cardus, Neville, *Australian Summer*, Jonathan Cape, London, 1937

Cardus, Neville, *English Cricket*, Collins, London, 1945

Cardus, Neville, *The Playfair Cardus,* Dickens Press, London, 1963

Carew, Dudley, *England Over,* Martin Secker, London, 1927

Carew, Dudley, *The Son of Grief,* Arthur Barker, London, 1936

Carew, Dudley, *To the Wicket,* Chapman & Hall, London, 1946

Fingleton, Jack, *Cricket Crisis,* Cassell, London, 1946

Fingleton, Jack, *Brown & Company: The Tour in Australia,* Collins, Sydney, 1951

Fingleton, Jack, *Masters of Cricket,* Heinemann, London, 1958

Giridhar, S. and V. J. Raghunath, *Mid-wicket Tales: From Trumper to Tendulkar,* Sage Publications, New Delhi, 2014

Guha, Ramachandra, *Spin and Other Turns: Indian Cricket's Coming of Age,* Penguin, New Delhi, 1994

Horan, Tom (writer), Pat Mullins and Brian Crowley (eds), *Cradle Days of Australian Cricket: An Anthology of the Writings of 'Felix' (T. P. Horan),* Macmillan, South Melbourne, 1989

James, C. L. R., *Beyond a Boundary,* Hutchinson, London, 1963

James, C. L. R., *Cricket,* Allison & Busby, London, 1989

Kippax, Alan and E. P. Barbour, *Anti Body-line,* Hurst & Blackett, London, 1933

Knight, Albert, *The Complete Cricketer,* Methuen, London, 1906

Martineau, G. D., *They Made Cricket,* Museum Press, London, 1956

Moult, Thomas (ed.), *Bat and Ball: A New Book of Cricket,* Arthur Barker, London, 1935

Moyes, A. G., *A Century of Cricketers,* Angus & Robertson, Sydney, 1950

Moyes, A. G., *Australian Batsmen: From Charles Bannerman to Neil Harvey,* Harrap, London, 1954

Moyes, A. G., *The Changing Face of Cricket,* Angus & Robertson, Sydney, 1963

Pycroft, James, *The Cricket Field: or, The History and the Science of the Game of Cricket,* Longmans, Green, Reader and Dyer, London, 1868

Stivens, Dal, *The Demon Bowler and Other Cricket Stories*, Outback Press, Collingwood, 1979

Thomson, A. A., *Cricket: The Golden Ages*, Stanley Paul, London, 1961

Trevor, Philip, *The Lighter Side of Cricket*, Methuen, London, 1901

Trevor, Philip, *The Problems of Cricket*, Sampson Low, London, 1907

Trevor, Philip, *Cricket and Cricketers*, Chapman & Hall, London, 1921

Whitington, R. S. and Keith Miller, *Straight Hit,* Latimer House, London, 1952

Whitington, R. S. and Keith Miller, *Bumper,* Latimer House, London, 1953

Whitington, R. S. and Keith Miller, *Cricket Typhoon,* Macdonald, London, 1955

Whitington, R. S., *Captains Outrageous?: Cricket in the Seventies*, Stanley Paul, London, 1972

## CRICKET: PICTORIAL

Alcock, Charles, *Famous Cricketers and Cricket Grounds,* Hudson & Kearns, London, 1895

Allen, David Rayvern, *Cricket: An Illustrated History*, Phaidon, Oxford, 1990

Anderson, Duncan, *Echoes from a Golden Age: Postcard Photographs of Cricketers by Foster and Hawkins,* Boundary Books, Childrey, 2010

Bouwman, Richard, *Glorious Innings: Treasures from the Melbourne Cricket Club Collection*, Hutchinson, Melbourne, 1987

Chadwick, Adam, *A Portrait of Lord's*, Scala Arts and Heritage, London, 2013

Dunstan, Keith, *The Tapestry Story: Celebrating 150 Years of the Melbourne Cricket Ground*, Lothian, South Melbourne, 2003

Eagar, Patrick (comp.), *Caught in the Frame: 150 Years of Cricket Photography,* CollinsWillow, London, 1992

Frith, David, *The Golden Age of Cricket, 1890–1914*, Lutterworth Press, Guildford, 1978

Frith, David, *Pageant of Cricket*, Macmillan, South Melbourne, 1987

Fry, C. B., *The Book of Cricket*, George Newnes, London, 1899

Green, Stephen, *Lord's: The Cathedral of Cricket*, Tempus, Gloucestershire, 2003

March, Russell (comp.), *The Cricketers of Vanity Fair*, Webb & Bower, Exeter, 1990

Ray, Mark (ed.), *Long Shadows: 100 Years of Australian Cricket*, Random House Australia, Sydney, 2006

Simon, Robin and Alastair Smart, *The Art of Cricket*, Secker & Warburg, London, 1983

Taylor, Alfred D., *The Story of a Cricket Picture (Sussex and Kent)*, self-published booklet, 1923

Whitington, R. S., *An Illustrated History of Australian Cricket*, Lansdowne Press, Melbourne, 1972

Wilkinson, Jack (comp.), *Great Australian Cricket Pictures*, Sun Books, Melbourne, 1975

Williams, Marcus and Gordon Phillips, *The Wisden Book of Cricket Memorabilia*, Lennard, Oxford, 1990


## GENERAL: PHOTOGRAPHY

Baldwin, Gordon, Malcolm Daniel and Sarah Greenough (eds), *All the Mighty World: The Photographs of Roger Fenton, 1852–1860*, Metropolitan Museum of Art, New York, 2004

Benjamin, Walter, *A Work of Art in the Age of Mechanical Reproduction*, Penguin, London, 2008

Berger, John, *Understanding a Photograph*, Penguin Classics, London, 2013

Bowers, Mike (ed.), *Century of Pictures: 100 Years of Herald Photography*, Penguin Viking, Camberwell, 2008

Crombie, Isobel, *Fred Kruger: Intimate Landscapes*, National Gallery of Victoria, Melbourne, 2012

Davies, Alan, *Eye for Photography: The Camera in Australia*, Melbourne University Publishing, Carlton, 2004

Gernsheim, Helmut (with Alison Gernsheim), *The History of Photography from the Camera Obscura to the Beginning of the Modern Era*, Thames & Hudson, London, 1969

Hannavy, John, *Roger Fenton of Crimble Hall*, Gordon Fraser Gallery, London, 1975

Klugman, Matthew and Gary Osmond, *Black and Proud: The Story of an Iconic AFL Photo*, NewSouth, Sydney, 2013

Lydon, Jane, *Eye Contact: Photographing Indigenous Australians*, Duke University Press, Durham, 2005

McCabe, Constance and Neal McCabe, *Baseball's Golden Age: The Photographs of Charles M. Conlon*, Abradale Press, New York, 1993

Morris, Errol, *Believing Is Seeing: Observations on the Mysteries of Photography*, Penguin, New York, 2011

Prodger, Philip (with an essay by Tom Gunning), *Time Stands Still: Muybridge and the Instantaneous Photography Movement*, Oxford University Press, Oxford, 2003

Solnit, Rebecca, *River of Shadows: Eadweard Muybridge and the Technological Wild West*, Viking, New York, 2003

## GENERAL: HISTORY

Adams, Francis, *Australian Life*, Chapman & Hall, London, 1892

Atkinson, Alan, *The Europeans in Australia: A History – Volume 3, Nation*, New South, Sydney, 2014

Cashman, Richard, *Sport in the National Imagination*, Walla Walla Press, Sydney, 2002

Cashman, Richard and Michael McKernan (eds), *Sport in History: The Making of Modern Sporting History*, UQP, St Lucia, 1979

Comettant, Oscar, *In the Land of Kangaroos and Gold Mines: A Frenchman's View of Australia in 1888*, Rigby, Adelaide, 1980

Dobbs, Brian, *Edwardians at Play*, Pelham, London, 1973

Finch-Hatton, Harold, *Advance Australia!: An Account of Eight Years' Work, Wandering and Amusement, in Queensland, New South Wales and Victoria*, W. H. Allen, London, 1886

Froude, J. A., *Oceana, or England and Her Colonies*, Longmans, Green, London, 1886

Harper, Melissa and Richard White (eds), *Symbols of Australia*, UNSW Press with National Museum of Australia Press, Sydney, 2010

Jalland, Pat, *Australian Ways of Death: A Social and Cultural History, 1840–1918*, Oxford University Press, Melbourne, 2002

Jalland, Pat, *Changing Ways of Death in Twentieth Century Australia: War, Medicine and the Funeral Business*, UNSW Press, Sydney, 2006

Kinglake, Edward, *The Australian at Home*, Leadenhall Press, London, 1892

McKernan, Michael, *The Australian People and the Great War*, Thomas Nelson, West Melbourne, 1980

Mandle, William, *Going It Alone: Australia's National Identity in the Twentieth Century*, Penguin, Ringwood, 1978

Souter, Gavin, *Lion & Kangaroo: The Initiation of Australia*, Text Publishing, Melbourne, 2000

Twopeny, Richard, *Town Life in Australia*, Elliot Stock, London, 1883

White, Richard, *Inventing Australia: Images and Identity 1688–1980*, Allen & Unwin, Sydney, 1981

## MISCELLANEOUS

[--------], 'Instructions for Using the Adams Videx Camera', Adams & Co, Charing Cross Road, London, 1907

Birkenhead, Second Earl of, *F. E.: The Life of F. E. Smith, First Earl of Birkenhead,* Eyre & Spottiswoode, London, 1960

Darwin, Charles, *The expression of the emotions in man and animals,* John Murray, London, 1872

Dennis, C. J., T*he Moods of Ginger Mick,* Angus & Robertson, Sydney, 1916

Ellis, Havelock, *A Study of British Genius,* Hurst & Blackett, London, 1904

FitzSimons, Peter, *Great Australian Sports Champions,* Harper Collins, Sydney, 2006

Galton, Francis, *Hereditary Genius: An Inquiry into Its Laws and Consequences,* Macmillan, London, 1869

Greenland, W. Kingscote (ed.), *Raymond Preston, British and Australian Evangelist: Life Story and Personal Reminiscences,* Epworth Press, London, 1930

Heseltine, Harry, *Vance Palmer,* UQP, St Lucia, 1970

Horne, Donald, *The Lucky Country: Australia in the Sixties,* Penguin, Ringwood, 1964

Hornung, E. W., *The Camera Fiend,* Scribner's Son, New York, 1911

Hornung, E. W., *The Collected Raffles,* Everyman Library, London, 1985

Housman, A. E., *A Shropshire Lad,* John Lane Company, New York, 1906

Hughes, Thomas, *Tom Brown's Schooldays,* Thomas Nelson & Sons, London, 1900

Lawson, Henry, *Poems,* with preface and chronology by Colin Roderick, John Ferguson, Sydney, 1979

McMahon, Darrin M., *Divine Fury: A History of Genius,* Basic Books, New York, 2013

Marshall, Ian, *The Undesirable Immigrant*, Temple House, Hartwell, 2006

Masson, Rosaline (ed.), *I Can Remember Robert Louis Stevenson*, Frederick Stokes, New York, 1922

Morris, Ronald, *The Indomitable Beatie: Charles Hoare, C. B. Fry and the Captain's Lady*, Sutton Publishing, Phoenix Mill, 2004

Musil, Robert, *The Man Without Qualities*, Vintage Books, New York, 1996

Myers, A. Wallis, *The Complete Lawn Tennis Player*, George Jacobs & Co, Philadelphia, 1908

Palmer, Geoffrey and Noel Lloyd, *E. F. Benson: As He Was*, Lennard, Luton, 1988

Palmer, Vance, *Intimate Portraits and Other Pieces*, Cheshire, Melbourne, 1969

Palmer, Vance, *The Swayne Family*, Angus & Robertson, Sydney, 1934

Souter, Gavin, *Company of Heralds: A Century and a Half of Australian Publishing by John Fairfax Limited and Its Predecessors*, Melbourne University Press, Carlton, 1981

Spencer, Thomas, *How McDougall Topped the Score and Other Verses and Sketches*, NSW Bookstall Co, Sydney, 1906

Stephens, A. G., *Victor Daley*, Bulletin Newspaper Co., Sydney, 1905

Taylor, J. H., *Golf: My Life's Work*, Jonathan Cape, London, 1943

Tennant, Kylie, *Foveaux*, Gollancz, London, 1939

Turner, Duncan, *A New Treatment of Consumption and Other Chronic Chest Diseases*, George Robertson, Melbourne, 1904

Wainwright, David and Catherine Dinn, *Henry Scott Tuke, 1858–1929, Under Canvas*, Sarema, London, 1989

Wallace, Catherine, *Catching the Light: The Art and Life of Henry Scott Tuke, 1858–1929*, Atelier Books, Edinburgh, 2008

## SELECTED JOURNAL ARTICLES AND BOOK CHAPTERS

Allison, Lincoln, 'Batsman and Bowler: The Key Relation of Victorian England', *Journal of Sport History*, Vol. 7, No. 2 (Summer 1980), pp. 5–20

Alomes, Stephen, 'Australian Nationalism in the Eras of Imperialism and "Internationalism"', *Australian Journal of Politics & History*, Vol. 34, Issue 3, December 1988, pp. 320–32

'C. G. K.', 'Science and Art of Cricket', *Nature*, Vol. 73, No. 1882, 23 November 1905, pp. 82–4

Cashman, Richard, 'Symbols of Unity: Anglo-Australian Cricketers, 1877–1900', *International Journal of the History of Sport*, Vol. 7, No. 1, 1990, pp. 97–110

Cunneen, Chris, 'Elevating and Recording the People's Pastimes: Sydney Sporting Journalism 1886–1939', in *Sport, Money, Morality and the Media*, edited by Richard Cashman and Michael McKernan, UNSW Press, Kensington, 1981

Goodwin, Clayton, 'The Aura of Celebrity', *The Lancet*, Vol. 363, No. 9409, 21 February 2004, p. 668

Haigh, Gideon, 'Top Shot That', *Portrait*, No. 34, Summer 2009, pp. 4–7

Haigh, Gideon, '"He Opened the Windows of the Mind": How Victor Trumper Changed the Way Australians See Cricket', Jack Marsh History Lecture 2015, Sydney Cricket Ground, 21 January 2015

Hanley, Howard, 'Silent Voices from the Lord's Pavilion', *The Yorker*, Issue 45, Spring 2011, pp. 17–22

Holt, Richard, 'Cricket and Englishness: The Batsman as Hero', *International Journal of the History of Sport*, Vol. 13, Issue 1, 1996, pp. 48–70

Judd, Barry, '"It's Not Cricket": Victorian Aboriginal Cricket at Coranderrk', *LaTrobe Journal*, No. 85, May 2010, pp. 37–54

McAuliffe, Chris, 'The Game of Nationhood: Art, Football and Australian Federation', *Journal of Australian Studies*, Vol. 37, No. 4, November 2013, pp. 520–34

Manning, Greg, 'The Cricketer as Galahad: A Sketch History of the Myth of Victor Trumper', unpublished

Mondy, Dave, 'How Things Break', *Iowa Review*, Vol. 44, Issue 3, Winter 2014/15

Phillips, Murray, 'Remembering Sport History: Narrative, Social Memory and the Origins of the Rugby League in Australia', *International Journal of the History of Sport*, Vol. 21, Issue 1, January 2004, pp. 50–66

Sharpham, Peter, 'The Origin of the Green and Gold', *Sporting Traditions*, Vol. 10, No. 2, pp. 21–8

Smith, Paul, 'Through a Glass, Brightly', *MCC Magazine*, Summer 2015, pp. 32–5

## AUDIOVISUAL MATERIAL

*Australian Cricketers on the Field in Cheltenham*, British Mutoscope and Biograph Company (1899), NFSA Title No: 1141013

*England v Australia 1905*, *British Movietone Digital Archive*, www.movietone.com

*Australian Cricketers Practice at Lord's*, Pathé Super Gazette (1930), NFSA Title No: 18477, fragments of recovered 1905 footage included in 1930 film

*Australia v South Africa, Test Match Cricket, Sydney*, Pathé Animated Gazette (1910), NFSA Title No: 817530

*The Last Innings of Victor Trumper: The Champion of Champions*, Australasian Gazette (1915), NFSA Title No: 66836

*That's Cricket*, Australasian Film (director: Ken G. Hall) (1931), NFSA Title No: 11010

*They Were Champions: Victor Trumper*, radio serial broadcast on 3DB
(December 1953), NFSA Title No: 246850

'Victor Trumper' from The Lucksmiths' album *Boondoggle*, Candle
Records (1994), NFSA Title No: 743256

## NEWSPAPERS, PERIODICALS AND ANNUALS

Australia: *The Advertiser, The Age, Albury Banner and Wodonga Express, The
Argus, The Arrow, The Australasian, The Australian, Australian Review
of Reviews, Australian Town and Country Journal, The Bulletin, Courier-
Mail, Daily Standard* (Brisbane), *Daily Telegraph, Gundagai Times,
The Herald, Inside Sport, Manly Daily, Meanjin, Mirror of Australia,
Newcastle Sun, Northern Star (Lismore), The Queenslander, The Referee,
Richmond River Express and Tweed Advertiser, Singleton Argus, Sporting
Globe, The Sportsman, The Sun, Sun-Herald, Sydney Mail, Sydney
Morning Herald, Table Talk, Wellington Times, West Australian.*

India: *Indian Cricket, Sport & Pastime, Wisden India*

New Zealand: *Christchurch Press, Young Man's Magazine*

United Kingdom: *Amateur Photographer, Athletic News, British Journal
of Photography, The Captain, C. B. Fry's Magazine of Action and
Outdoor Life, Cricket: A Weekly Record of the Game, The Cricketer, Daily
Chronicle, Daily Express, Daily Graphic, Daily Mail, Daily Telegraph
(London), Daily Telegraph (Sheffield), Derby Daily Telegraph,
Edinburgh Evening Post, Evening News, Evening Standard, The Field,
Golf Illustrated, The Graphic, Hull Daily Mail, Illustrated London News,
Illustrated Sporting and Dramatic News, Manchester Courier, Manchester
Evening News, Manchester Guardian, New Review, News of the
World, Nottingham Evening Post, Sporting Gazette, Sporting Life, The
Sportsman, Strand Magazine, Sunday Times, Times Literary Supplement,
Vanity Fair, Voice of the Century, Wisden Cricketers' Almanack*

# IMAGE CREDITS

Author's Collection viii, 12–13, 46, 47, 100 (both), 103, 266, 272, 278 (all), 285

Beldam Collection 132 (all), 137 (all), 139, 282

Andrew Bernard 226

Max Bonnell 54

Boundary Books 89, 91, 114, 134, 216

British Newspaper Archive 64, 78

Philip Brown 290

Cricket NSW 191, 201

Eadweard Muybridge Online Archive 93

Fairfax Photos 288

Steve Flemming 147 (right)

David Frith 69

John Hawkins 144

Arthur Mailey Jnr 170

Melbourne Cricket Club 3, 7 (both), 9, 15, 18, 25, 37, 95, 97, 147 (left), 154, 196, 225, 237, 264 (all)

Estate of David Moore 260

National Library of Australia 123

National Portrait Gallery xvi

Michael Ryan 182 (left)

Peter Schofield 182 (right)

State Library of Victoria 20, 166, 207, 230, 250

## PICTURE SECTION

Author's Collection 3 (top and middle), 14 (middle left),
     15 (middle right and bottom right)

Russell Ayres 14 (bottom right)

Beldam Collection 4 (all), 7 (all)

Andrew Bernard 9 (bottom)

Boundary Books 11 (bottom left)

British Library 8

Peter Brown 12 (top left)

Judith Dobie 14 (top left)

Hardie Grant 11 (bottom right)

John Hawkins 15 (top left and top right)

*The Hindu* 13 (middle right)

Ian Kenins 12 (bottom)

Marylebone CC 1 (bottom)

Melbourne CC 2 (bottom), 3 (bottom), 5, 6 (top),
     10 (top left and bottom right), 11 (top left and top right),
     12 (top right), 15 (middle left)

National Film and Sound Archive 2 (top right), 9 (top)

National Library of Australia 13 (top)

National Portrait Gallery 10 (top right)

Newspix 16 (bottom)

Jim Pavlidis 16 (top)

Tim Rogers 13 (bottom left)

Peter Schofield 2 (top left)

State Library of Victoria 1 (top)

Surrey CCC 6 (bottom)

Dave Thomas 14 (bottom left)

Balaji Venugopal 13 (bottom right)

Peter Young 14 (top right)

# ACKNOWLEDGEMENTS

The origins of *Stroke of Genius* lie in a talk, the Jack Marsh Memorial Lecture, delivered at the Sydney Cricket & Sports Ground Trust in January 2015: '"He Opened the Windows of the Mind": How Victor Trumper Changed the Way Australians Saw Cricket'. I should therefore first doff my cap to Rodney Cavalier, former chairman of the Sydney Cricket Ground Trust, for his invitation, and to museum staff Leah Domanski and Anthony O'Carroll for making the presentation possible. The book was then put together in and around various contemporary cricket commitments, including an Ashes series scheduled for thirty days which lasted eighteen, enabling invaluable visits on Michael Down and John Hawkins, Lord's and The Oval, and the pleasure of connecting with descendants of the co-authors of *Great Batsmen: Their Methods at a Glance*: George Beldam's daughter-in-law Cornelia, and C. B. Fry's grandson Jonathan and his wife Marilyn. Throughout this period I was most generously hosted by Mike Atherton and Isabelle de Caires: as ever, I am in their debt.

For help too extensive to enumerate fully, I should like to thank: Marie-Louise and Russell Ayres, Andrew Bernard, Max Bonnell, Keith Booth, Neal Bryson, Andy Bull, Stephanie Bunbury, Colin Clowes, Liz Conor, Kaz Cooke, Dennis Coon, Jennifer Cornwall, Brad Diebert, Judith Dobie, Marty Donald, Elizabeth Edwards, Michael Fahey, David Frith, Glenn Gibson, John and Jeremy Goff,

Ramachandra Guha, Howard Hanley, Graeme Haigh, John Harms, Philippa Hawker, the Rt Hon John Howard, Russell Jackson, Ian Kenins, Damien Kingsbury, Louis Laumen, Reg Lynch, Chris McAuliffe, David McLachlan, Greg Manning, James Merchant, Mark Mordue, Wayne Owens, Jim Pavlidis, Dileep Premachandran, Mark Ray, Tim Rice, Tim Rogers, Christian Ryan, Peter Schofield, Graem Sims, John Spooner, David Strange, Roger Taylor, Dave Thomas, Richard Warlow, Robert Willcocks, Peter Young. S. Giridhar introduced me to Balaji Venugopal; Clayton Murzello was kind enough to put me in contact with Vasant Raiji. Important advice and assistance on matters of photography came from Bob Thomas, Patrick Eagar, Philip Brown, Paul Smith, Eric Evans and a correspondent at www.earlyphotography.co.uk who remained anonymous despite answering in great detail my many questions about the workings of the Adam Videx.

Whatever's wrong with *Stroke of Genius* is my fault; any credit I must share with the personnel of Penguin Random House Australia who cared mightily for the book at every stage. Ben Ball was an exceptional publisher. Rachel Scully, Jeremy Sherlock and Samantha Jayaweera were tireless helpmates through the immense design challenge of marrying text and image. Katie Purvis was an attentive editor. Writing is a lonely business; I warmly appreciated the company.

I further acknowledge the assistance of staff of the National Library of Australia, the National Museum of Australia, the State Libraries of Victoria, South Australia, New South Wales and Queensland, the British Library, London Metropolitan Archives and the Surrey History Centre, Siobhan Dee and Sean Bridgman from the National Film and Sound Archive, Audrey Snell at the All England Tennis Club, Neil Robinson, Heather Thomas and Robert

ACKNOWLEDGEMENTS

Curphey at Marylebone Cricket Club. Above all, felicitations to David Studham, Trevor Ruddell, Steve Flemming and April West at the Melbourne Cricket Club, who were tireless, tactful and brought to my attention much I may otherwise have missed. The burden of living with a tired and taciturn Trumper obsessive, meanwhile, was nobly borne by my wife Charlotte and daughter Cecilia. Thanks to them, and apologies for my endless preoccupation.